STUDIES IN
MARK'S GOSPEL

A. T. Robertson

Late Professor of New Testament Interpretation,
Southern Baptist Theological Seminary, Louisville,
Kentucky

Revised and Edited by Heber F. Peacock

BROADMAN PRESS
Nashville, Tennessee

Dewey Decimal Classification: 226.3
Library of Congress card catalog number 58-8925
Printed in the United States of America

Preface

The chapters of this book first appeared as articles during the year 1918 in the following publications: *The Biblical World, The Constructive Quarterly, The Convention Teacher, The Expositer, The Homiletic Review, The Methodist Review,* and *The Sunday School Times.* Thanks are hereby returned to the several publishers for permission to republish them in book form. The chapters have all been carefully revised and, in some instances, changed to suit the present purpose. They cover many aspects of the Gospel without attempting full and formal exposition. It is hoped that by this method a wider circle of readers may be reached.

This Gospel has the charm of two personalities who contributed to its contents—Peter and John Mark. Both were vivacious and versatile and have preserved the portrait of Jesus with the freshness of the morning. Modern criticism of the Gospels finds in Mark's book the foundation (along with the Logia of Jesus) of the other three. It is impossible to overestimate the critical and historical worth of the Second Gospel, which is really the first in order of time. Professor J. Rendel Harris tells us that the eternal youth of Jesus was one of the charms that the Master has for mystics. In this Gospel Jesus fascinates us with the vigor of young manhood and the glory of the Godhead. The present volume turns the picture around so that it may be seen from this angle and from that. But the eye of Jesus holds us enthralled all the while with his pity and his power.

A. T. ROBERTSON

Editor's Foreword

Some forty years have passed since these chapters were first written. During that period major advances have been made in the area of Gospel studies, especially in the Gospel of Mark. The period has seen the appearance of new theories and solutions to the Synoptic problem, the rise of the form-critical method, the resurgence of biblical theology, and the appearance of numerous commentaries and special studies on the Gospel of Mark.

This book has, however, not outlived its usefulness. It was not, and is not, presented as a major contribution to the field of Marcan scholarship. It is intended to be a sane and practical guide to the study of Mark. It is hoped that pastor and layman alike will find help here in understanding and interpreting the beginning of the gospel of Jesus Christ.

The editor has limited his work of revision to the correction of apparent errors, the elimination of technical language, and the reduction of the number of references to long-dead controversies and literature. He has deleted nothing essential; he has added nothing of importance.

HEBER F. PEACOCK

Louisville, Kentucky

Contents

I

The Making of John Mark

Barnabas and Saul returned from Jerusalem . . . ,
taking with them John whose surname was Mark.
ACTS 12:25.*

John Mark, the author of the Second Gospel, has absolutely nothing to say about himself in his Gospel, unless there is a veiled reference in 14:51 f., where we have the elusive figure of "a certain young man" who followed Jesus to Gethsemane and who fled, leaving his loose night robe, when the officers arrested the Master. This may be John Mark, the son of Mary, in whose house the disciples met at a later time (Acts 12:12). If so, it was at his mother's house that Jesus partook of the last Passover meal. But Papias says that Mark was not a personal follower of Jesus.

1. *Glimpses of Mark.*—However, we do get a good many glimpses of John Mark in Acts and in Paul's epistles. By means of these we can form some idea of the young man who performed such a great work in the writing of the Gospel that lies at the basis of both Matthew and Luke, according to the almost unanimous opinion of modern scholars. For every reason, therefore, modern Christians are interested in Mark. It is not the purpose of this chapter to discuss the sources of Mark's information, though Papias is almost certainly correct in his statement, on the authority of the Elder, that Mark was the disciple and interpreter of Simon Peter

* All Scripture references are quoted from the American Standard Version.

and wrote down Peter's discourses about our Lord. Luke tells us (1:1–4) that he made use of both oral and written sources. There is no reason to think that Mark confined himself to what Peter said, when he had access to other disciples also who flocked to his mother's house in Jerusalem (Acts 12:12). But in this chapter we are concerned with Mark himself and some of the things that went into the making of this useful servant of Christ.

2. *Not a Man of the Highest Gifts.*—There are undoubted advantages in being a man of supreme genius like Paul or John the evangelist. But these men are few, and the great majority must take a lower place. All the evidence goes to show that Mark was a young man of good, but not unusual, native gifts. Most of the work of the world is done by men of this type. The love of work is after all a form of genius, better than mere brilliance of intellect. At first Mark did not seem to have this application to hard tasks. He did not quickly find himself, and he seemed fickle.

3. *On Making Mistakes.*—He was the kind of man to be the victim of moods and of whims, and so to make mistakes. Now, mistakes are not a desirable asset in any man's character, though no one of us is wholly free from them. It is human to err, and we stumble in spite of all that we can do. Least of all is the habit of making mistakes to be cultivated. Some mistakes are more or less venial, but others are fatal. Some mistakes can be overcome. Some of us learn by our mistakes and make them steppingstones to God. John Mark had a great experience that affected his whole career.

4. *Mark's Good Start.*—His youthful environment was good, for at his mother's home he met constantly the leading spirits of early Christianity. Here were to be seen frequently the twelve apostles, James the brother of Jesus, Barnabas the cousin of Mark, Mary the mother of Jesus, the other women, Philip the deacon-evangelist, and many others

2

whose names we do not know. It is a great education for young people to live in a home where the great and good of earth meet. Mark's mother was clearly a woman of talent and left her impress upon her boy, who was to bring her undying fame. At first Mark was the son of Mary, but by and by Mary was known as the mother of John Mark. This was as she would have wished it to be, as any mother wishes it to be who finds her jewels in her children.

Mark was fortunate also in the love and friendship of Barnabas, who was always on the lookout for young men whom he could help. Paul was one of those whom Barnabas befriended at Jerusalem when all the disciples looked askance at this new sheep in the flock which had so lately ravened as a wolf. They fancied that they could still see the wolf's ears beneath the sheep's clothing (Acts 9:26 f.). So Barnabas took along John Mark to Antioch when he and Saul returned thither from Jerusalem (Acts 12:25). Mark may not have taken the enterprise very seriously. At any rate, the Holy Spirit called upon Barnabas and Saul to go upon the first great campaign to win the Gentiles to Christ (Acts 13:1-3). The Greek church at Antioch rose to the occasion and gave their blessing to the movement.

It was for this hour that Saul had longed and looked since Christ set him apart to go "far hence to the Gentiles," though he had by no means been idle during the intervening years. But even so, the company went out with Barnabas still the leader, as he had brought Saul from Tarsus to Antioch (Acts 11:25). But John Mark seems to have been taken along in some sort of subordinate position that is not made clear by the reference in Acts 13:5, "They had also John as their attendant." The Greek word means "under-rower" on a ship, down below the ranks of "upper-rowers." It was sometimes employed for the synagogue minister or attendant, as in Luke 4:20. It is not necessary to know precisely what Mark

3

was expected to do. He may have been advance agent to arrange about the hotels, meeting places, means of travel, and so on. He may have done the baptizing and helped talk to the inquirers (the catechumens). Clearly his work was subordinate to that of Barnabas and Saul. But many another young man has had his opportunity by beginning in a humble way. Men prove themselves worthy of bigger things by doing well the smaller task in hand.

5. *Mark's Failure in a Crisis.*—It seems clear that Mark had no idea of the real greatness of Paul at this juncture. To his thinking, Barnabas was the greater man, and he may have resented the sudden leadership of Paul at Paphos. It was now "Paul and his company" (Acts 13:13) that set sail from Paphos and that came to Perga in Pamphylia. It was at Perga that matters came to a crisis with Mark. He may have been a bit irritated at his subordinate place, and all the more now that Paul had displaced Barnabas as the head of the party. It seems clear that something happened at Perga that Luke has not recorded. Ramsay thinks that Paul had an attack of malaria at this coast town. Mark may also have been the victim of the mosquito. Depression seized Mark, who may not have cared to face the perils of rivers and perils of robbers that lay ahead of the party on the high tablelands of Pisidia and Lycaonia (the southern part of the province of Galatia). Paul seemed bent on pushing on in this campaign, and Barnabas stood by him. Mark apparently had had no specific call from the Holy Spirit for this enterprise and so felt less responsibility in the matter, though he had joined hands with the company.

At any rate, at Perga "John departed from them and returned to Jerusalem" (Acts 13:13). In this incidental way Luke notes the defection of Mark. He did not go to Antioch, where it would be embarrassing to make explanations, but to his home in Jerusalem. Probably Mark felt that the

4

reasons for his course were excellent and fully justified his conduct. It is not difficult to find reasons in plenty for not doing a hard and disagreeable task. Paul and Barnabas faced the dangers ahead and pressed on, and, "passing through from Perga, came to Antioch of Pisidia" (Acts 13:14) and made this journey one of the epochal events in history, for it led to the evangelization of the Graeco-Roman world and the liberation of Christianity, after a struggle, from the fetters that the Judaizers tried to impose upon it (Acts 11:1–18; 15:1–35). One of the tests of a man's fiber is to know when a crisis has come. Mark took his defection rather lightly, but Paul took it much to heart.

6. *Paul's Indignation at Mark's Conduct.*—The explosion came about in a rather incidental way after the return of Paul and Barnabas and after their victory over the Judaizers at the Jerusalem conference. The Judaizers were alarmed at the rapid spread of Christianity among the Gentiles as a result of this tour and challenged the validity of the work of Paul and Barnabas, demanding that these Gentile Christians become Jews (Acts 15:1 f.). Thus one of the greatest issues in the history of Christianity was sprung. To yield was to make Christianity a sect of current pharisaic Judaism. It was the real spiritual Israel, and Paul and Barnabas were not going to allow such a calamity to befall the Gentile churches as these pharisaic Christians from Jerusalem planned. Peter, James, and John (Gal. 2:9) stood by Paul in Jerusalem (Acts 15:4–29) so that Paul and Barnabas returned to Antioch in triumph (Acts 15:30–35).

Nothing is said of Mark, but it is quite possible that he at this juncture was indifferent to Paul's contention. Indeed, later Peter came to Antioch and followed Paul and Barnabas in practicing social equality with the Greek Christians and then drew back (Gal. 2:11 f.) because some Judaizers from Jerusalem threatened more trouble to Peter (cf. Acts 11:1–18), claiming that James was against the present attitude of Peter on this phase of the question. Peter's defection induced even Barnabas to desert Paul in this "dissimulation" (hypocrisy).

It is possible that Mark's coolness toward Paul may have caused Barnabas to weaken for the moment and to leave Paul. At any rate, Paul rebuked Peter and Barnabas and won them back to his side. The time came when Paul proposed to Barnabas that they "return now and visit the brethren in every city wherein we proclaimed the word of the Lord, and see how they fare" (Acts 15:36). Barnabas was more than willing but suggested that they take along with them John Mark. Instantly the long-smoldering indignation of Paul burst forth: "But Paul thought not good to take with them him who withdrew from them from Pamphylia, and went not with them to the work" (Acts 15:38). Paul's word for "withdrew" is literally "apostatized." And, then, Mark had not stuck to the work. He had flickered in a crisis. Paul had no intention of taking Mark back again over the same ground. The mosquitoes were still at Perga. Luke uses the imperfect tense to express Paul's stubborn resistance to the plan of Barnabas. We are not told more of the conversation, but Luke adds that "there arose a sharp contention" (paroxysm). Probably sharp things were said, so sharp that Paul and Barnabas "parted asunder one from the other." Paul cared too much for the work to risk a young man who would not stand true when the pinch came. He wished no deserters and no slackers with him.

7. *Mark's Second Chance with Barnabas.*—Barnabas practiced the gospel of the second chance and was determined that his cousin, John Mark, should have another opportunity to show what he could do. One is bound to admit that sympathy goes with Barnabas in this position, however much judgment may be with Paul. Barnabas took Mark with

him to Cyprus, his old home and possibly the original home of Mark's family. Paul went his way with Silas back to the scene of the first tour in Lycaonia and Pisidia. Paul and Barnabas agreed to disagree. Luke follows the fortunes of Paul, so that we know nothing more of Barnabas and Mark. We may be sure that Barnabas would demand that Mark be true this time. It is possible that this sharp rebuff by Paul did much to awaken Mark to a proper realization of his responsibility. Once more we may note how fortunate Mark was in having a friend like Barnabas, with the patience and the love to help him through his time of probation. Some of the early writers say that Mark went on to Egypt finally and did a great work there, but of this we know nothing definite. We do know how wise and gentle was Barnabas, the son of consolation.

8. *Making Good with Simon Peter.*—Peter himself bears witness to this fact in his first epistle (1 Pet. 5:13) when he speaks of "Mark my son" as with him "in Babylon" (probably Rome). The early writers testify that Mark was with Peter in Rome, that he was Peter's interpreter or dragoman, translating his Aramaic discourses into the current Greek. It is the common tradition that Mark wrote his Gospel with the discourses of Peter as the main source. Some say that he wrote at Peter's dictation; others, with his approval; others, after his death. But the testimony is unanimous, and internal evidence confirms it, that Mark faithfully preserved the substance of Peter's discourses about the Lord Jesus. Thus under Peter's tutelage he rendered a service of supreme worth for all the ages. He kept the lifelike touches of Peter's speeches and lets us see Jesus with Peter's keen eyes.

9. *A Comfort to Paul.*—It is good to know that Paul recognized that Mark had made good and could now be depended on to do his work. It is not incredible that Paul may have read Mark's Gospel while in Rome during his first

imprisonment. We know that Mark was here with Paul part of the time and that Paul was pleased with him. "Aristarchus my fellow-prisoner saluteth you, and Mark, the cousin of Barnabas (touching whom ye received commandments; if he come unto you, receive him)" (Col. 4:10). In the loneliness of the last imprisonment in Rome Paul begs Timothy, who is now in Asia, to come and "take Mark, and bring him with thee; for he is useful to me for ministering" (2 Tim. 4:11). Paul revised his judgment about Mark after he had noticed the change in his conduct. Probably Paul refers here to his experience with Mark in Rome (Col. 4:10). Paul was only too glad to give praise instead of blame.

Mark is a comfort to many a young man who has made a serious blunder in life. Take heart and wake up to the stern realities of duty. The war times brought us all up with a jerk. The main things of life called for our energy, and we learned to hold ourselves to the chief tasks. Most of us make slips. Most of us are not greatly gifted. But all of us can make our lives count for God by sticking steadily to the work to which we are called and to which we have put our hands. It is doubtless true that Mark's mistake at Perga and the sharp contention at Antioch served to rouse him to genuine exertion. Strenuous application took the place of indifference, and the result was victory.

II

The Date of Mark's Gospel

*Many have taken in hand to draw up a narrative
concerning those matters which have been fulfilled
among us.*   LUKE 1:1.

1. *Effect of the Two-Document Hypothesis.*—The interest of the world of New Testament scholarship has been
centered for some time upon the Second Gospel as one of
the two documents (Q and Mark) used by Matthew and
Luke for the major part of their Gospels. Critics are not
quite unanimous on this solution of the Synoptic problem,
but the majority of scholars do agree that something similar
to the Two-Document Hypothesis is necessary. In any case,
the date of Mark is still a matter of debate and of importance.

The general effect of the Two-Document Hypothesis has
been to push Mark back to a comparatively early date. If
we admit the use of Mark by Luke, this seems necessary.
Even those who would not agree to all the implications of
the hypothesis, especially in regard to the use of a second
source for Matthew and Luke, are willing to admit that
Mark was used in the other two Synoptic Gospels.

2. *The Date of Luke's Gospel.*—The argument is therefore part of a chain, the links of which hang together. If we
can determine the date of the composition of the Gospel
of Luke we may arrive at a conclusion in regard to the date
of Mark. It is a reasonable explanation for the close of Acts

9

that events had at that time proceeded no further. The concluding verses of Acts, together with the fact that the book gives no indication of the result of the trial of Paul or his martyrdom, make it quite probable that the work was written at a time when Paul's trial in Rome had not yet come to an end.

Since Luke wrote his Gospel before Acts, as he himself says (Acts 1:1), the first question is the date of Paul's release from his first Roman imprisonment. It is not certain that Nero passed on the case or that it came to trial. But whether Paul was dismissed without trial or set free after trial, it could not be later than A.D. 63. In any case, we may allow some three years (the year of the voyage and two in Rome) between the completion of the Gospel of Luke in Caesarea, where Paul with Luke spent two years (Acts 24:27), and the events recorded at the close of Acts. That would place the writing of the Gospel about A.D. 56–58. It is not necessary to date the Gospel of Luke so long before and to place its composition in Caesarea, though this is the natural thing to do, for while in Palestine, Luke had the time and the opportunity to procure the data which he used (Luke 1:1–4). Luke may have completed his Gospel in Rome. This is the conclusion of several scholars. If it is correct, it would indicate that both books of this great first-century historian were written while Paul was alive and still a prisoner in Rome.

It is clear that if this line of argument is correct, Mark's Gospel must come not later than A.D. 60 and probably earlier. Today many scholars agree that the Gospel of Mark could not have been written in its present form later than the sixth decade of the first century. This is in full accord with the line of argument presented by Hobart on the medical language of Luke to show that he was a man practiced in the scientific language of Greek medicine.

3. *The Date of Q.*—If we seek the earliest probable date and not the latest, we are at once confronted with Q (the other main source of Matthew and Luke, composed mainly of the sayings of Jesus), which was apparently earlier than Mark. Indeed, many scholars find in Mark traces of the use of Q. The whole question of the limits of Q is involved, but it cannot be discussed here. It is enough to say that we are not justified in confining Q solely to what is preserved in Matthew and Luke. We may admit that Mark shows some use of Q. We hold, therefore, that Mark knew and used Q, but only to a limited extent. If so, then Mark is later than Q. There are, however, those who oppose the idea that Mark knew and used Q.

But what is the date of this source? It cannot be proved, but it seems likely that there was a considerable interval of time between the original composition of Q and its use by Matthew and Luke. It is probable that the publication of the Gospel of Mark is the transition link which made possible the production of Matthew and Luke. A number of scholars hold that Q was written twenty or more years before Mark, and some hold that Q was actually written during the ministry of Jesus, since it stops short of the events of Passion Week. Others hold that the absence of references to the Passion Week is to be explained on the basis of the eager expectation of the nearness of the Parousia. They place the date of composition some few years after the death of Jesus. Indeed, the common use of shorthand during this period makes it possible that Q, although composed some years after the death of Jesus, contained actual shorthand reports of the sayings of Jesus. If we place Q at A.D. 42 and Luke's Gospel at A.D. 58, we seem to have the limits for Mark's Gospel. It is interesting to note how the most sincere and reliable Synoptic criticism points to an early date for Mark's Gospel.

4. *Matthew's Use of Mark.*—If Matthew's Greek Gospel made use of Mark, as is now generally admitted, though some voices insist that Mark made use of the Aramaic Matthew, the argument for the early date of Mark is made still stronger. In spite of the contention of some critics that Mark made use of the Aramaic Matthew, the majority of scholars continue to hold that the authors of the First and Third Gospels made use of the Gospel of Mark as one of their main sources. It is not necessary to show that Luke made use of Matthew to prove the early date of Mark's Gospel.

5. *The "Aramaic" Mark.*—A few scholars propose a still earlier date for Mark's Gospel in an Aramaic form. They hold that a very suitable date would be about A.D. 44 when Peter, who had been prominent as a leader of the church at Jerusalem, was obliged to leave the city. But the whole question of the Aramaic original of a Greek Gospel of Mark is quite uncertain. I fact, I am inclined to agree with the judgment of others that a translator would hardly give both the transliteration and the translation of the Aramaic. An effort is made to overcome this point by suggesting that Mark himself wrote the Aramaic while he was with Peter in Jerusalem about A.D. 44 and that he made the translation while with Paul and Barnabas at Antioch about A.D. 50. I do not care to discuss here the view that the original Mark was in Aramaic. The point that is pertinent is that the date of the Greek Mark seems to be as early as A.D. 50.

6. *Possible Editions by Mark.*—It is true that some of the early Christian writers suggest Rome as the place where the Gospel of Mark was written. Papias, however, has nothing as to the place of writing. Harnack examines with care all these traditions and concludes, "Tradition asserts no veto against the hypothesis that St. Luke, when he met St. Mark in the company of St. Paul the prisoner was permitted by him to peruse a written record of the Gospel history which

was essentially identical with the Gospel of St. Mark which was given to the Church at a later time." Harnack suggests, therefore, that Mark made a "final revision" of his work in Rome. There is nothing incongruous in the idea that Mark revised his Gospel once or twice. Indeed, it has been held that Mark wrote one edition of his Gospel at Caesarea, a shorthand report of Peter's sermon (Acts 10:34 ff.), another later in Egypt, and another in Rome.

It is not necessary to pass finally on these suggestions. They all go to show how criticism has cautiously felt its way in the study of the Gospel sources. All that needs to be said is that the question of editorial revision has not been settled and is still open for further study. I am convinced of the unity of the Gospel and of the Marcan authorship. Mark was with Peter in Jerusalem (Acts 12:12) and later in Rome ("Babylon," 1 Pet. 5:13), and possibly at other times. If his Gospel, as Papias said, rests primarily on the preaching of Peter, there is ample room for it in the early period. There is nothing to support the tradition in Irenaeus that Mark wrote after Peter's death.

7. *The Editing of Redactors.*—Several theories dealing with the editorial work of redactors call for brief remark. The view of Wendling on the origin of the Gospel of Mark, in spite of the keen insight and acuteness of literary analysis by which the theory is supported, must be rejected. His reconstruction of three stages in the creation of the Gospel, with the final stage being essentially our Gospel of Mark, has the merit of ingenuity and plausibility, but the elaborate structure must be dismantled. It has forced the facts into a preconceived pattern.

The Ur-Marcus theory still appeals to some minds, and it is suggested by Moffatt that there should be hesitation not in the acceptance but in the working out of the hypothesis that the canonical Mark, written shortly after A.D. 70, is based for the most part on a primitive Mark made up of Petrine reminiscences. The canonical Mark is usually considered to be the work of a redactor who made use of the Petrine reminiscenes which had been written by John Mark. The theory is frequently supported by appeal to the tradition of Irenaeus that "Mark," considered by proponents of this theory as the pseudonym of the redactor, wrote after the death of Peter. On the other hand, the divergent form of the tradition in Clement of Alexandria is rejected as an attempt to bring the writing under the imprimatur of Peter without making him responsible for all its contents.

The conclusion that these contradictory traditions leave us free to settle the date of Mark's Gospel apart from the stories in Irenaeus and Clement of Alexandria seems more plausible. It is hard to feel the force of an argument which rests upon the testimony of Irenaeus, who is contradicted by Clement of Alexandria, Origen, Eusebius, Epiphanius, and Jerome. When the theory of a redactor, using the materials of an Ur-Marcus, has become a certainty in the mind of the critic, Mark, of course, must be dated quite late to conform with the supposed facts. On the whole, there seems to be no compelling argument for the assumption of an Ur-Marcus. All the evidence points in the direction of the use of Mark's Gospel essentially as we have it by the authors of the First and Third Gospels.

8. *The Narrow Limits.*—It cannot be said that the Synoptic problem is settled. No problem in human knowledge is ever settled so that no intellect can raise objections to it. J. M. Robertson has a new book, *The Jesus Problem,* in which he seeks to show that Jesus never existed and is only a myth of the imagination. But Maurice Jones represents most scholars when he introduces his treatment of the Synoptic problem with this sentence: "The most notable achievement in the department of recent New Testament criticism

is undoubtedly the fairly general agreement arrived at with regard to the mutual relations of the first three Gospels."

It is not claimed that modern scholars are agreed as to the date of Mark's Gospel, only that a very late date is no longer contended for. As we have seen, the critics range from A.D. 44 to A.D. 75. Those who contend for the later date (A.D. 70–75) argue mainly from Mark 13, which is made to depend on a "Little Apocalypse" circulated among the Jews at the time of the destruction of Jerusalem and incorporated into the Second Gospel. But it is equally possible that the hypothetical "Little Apocalypse" was a report of the discourse of Jesus on the Mount of Olives, as it purports to be, which was used by Mark. There is no real reason for thinking that Mark confined his Gospel to his own notes or recollections of Peter's discourses. He may have employed Q. He probably used oral and written sources as did Luke. Certainly the position of Mark in Jerusalem made it easy for him to learn the current interpretation of Jesus among the disciples.

Luke himself in his Gospel (1:1–4) should have taught us all long ago that the writing of the sayings and deeds of Jesus began very early, for he spoke of many such attempts. Perhaps most of them were more or less incomplete or gave only detached incidents or reports of single discourses or parables. The Oxyrhynchus Logia of Jesus furnish a partial parallel to Q. Somewhere between 40 and 60, I should say, Mark wrote his Gospel substantially as we have it now and in Greek. It seems to me that the evidence as a whole points to 50 as the probable date.

9. *The Early Date Most Probable.*—At any rate, we can be grateful for the critical unanimity with which the priority of Mark is acknowledged and the correspondingly early date of this Gospel. It is worth all that it has cost to reach solid ground here. There is general agreement that in the

Gospel of Mark we have an early attempt to combine the isolated written and oral reminiscences of the ministry of Jesus which were available at the time.

The evidence on the whole demands an early date. This date is consonant with the character of the Gospel which preserves the lifelike touches from the preaching of Peter and allows some use of Q and other data from various sources with a few editorial touches some years later either by Mark himself, as is most likely, or by an editor. In Mark's Gospel, therefore, we catch the very atmosphere of the first generation of those who walked with Jesus over the hills and plains of Galilee. The note of wonder runs all through the Gospel of Mark. The people are seen all aglow with excitement in the presence of Jesus, the wonder-worker. Peter preserves the freshness of that early morn of Christianity. Mark himself is full of it and makes abundant use of the historical present tense as he visualizes the glory and rapture of those early days of the kingdom of God on earth. The frequent use of the imperfect tense is to the same effect. It is as if a motion-picture camera had filmed the moving crowds as they thronged about Jesus and followed him from place to place. The picture is toned down in Matthew and Luke, but in Mark the negative has the lines in the picture still. It is no wonder that children are fond of Mark's Gospel, for they can see Mark's picture of Jesus, and their eyes sparkle as they behold Him.

III

Mark's Gospel and the Synoptic Problem

It seemed good to me also, having traced the course of all things accurately from the first, to write unto thee in order, most excellent Theophilus; that thou mightest know the certainty concerning the things wherein thou wast instructed. LUKE 1:3–4.

The story of Jesus still fascinates the minds of men in spite of all efforts to relegate it to the limbo of myth or legend. Strauss and Renan failed to remove the Gospels from the sphere of serious historical documents. Drews and Smith likewise failed completely to destroy the historical character of Jesus. The tragic events of the twentieth century have shaken the world out of whatever indifference to Christ had come. Men are today face to face with Christ in a new and wonderful sense.

1. *The Necessity of Knowing Mark.*—The religious world is right up against the credibility and origin of the Gospel narratives. Right across one's path in the pursuit of this inquiry lies the Gospel of Mark. There can be no claim to an open-minded consideration of the historical basis of the Christian faith until one has taken some pains to apply the ordinary processes of historical criticism to the Gospel of Mark, the earliest extant form of the Gospel story. Mark's Gospel challenges the interest of the average man and of

the expert in New Testament literature. Indeed, some of the critics find in Mark the only historical basis for crediting the story of Jesus Christ. This view is certainly one-sided and incorrect, but it does serve to indicate the supreme significance of Mark for the historical critic and the theologian. Mark must be taken into account.

We wish to know, then, what scientific research has to say about Mark's Gospel. We have heard a great deal about the alleged unhistorical character of the Fourth Gospel as compared with the Synoptic Gospels. We have heard much also concerning the "Jesus or Christ controversy" as it raged around the Synoptic Gospels. In fact, however, we find "Christ" in the Synoptic Gospels as surely as we do in Paul. We are told to discount Paul as the one who, through his pharisaic rabbinism on the one hand and his Hellenism and mystery-religion affinities on the other, had perverted the simple gospel of the kingdom preached by Jesus. So we are told to go "back to Christ" and away from Paul. But now the Synoptic Gospels are said to be as guilty of theology as Paul. The discussion has even been turned to the Paulinism of Mark and the influence of Paul on the Fourth Gospel. The truth of these assumptions has yet to be proved. What does emerge, and rightly so, is the necessity of interpreting these documents in the light of the historical situation out of which they were written. We must seek to know what event gave rise to the story and through what phases the tradition passed to acquire its canonical forms. We have a duty to the Gospel, as to every other ancient document, to interpret it in the light of its own times.

2. *The Modern Versus the Traditional View of Mark.*— What, then, is Mark's Gospel in the light of modern criticism? The book has absolutely nothing to say about itself or its author. It is thus different from the Gospel of John (John 20:30 f.; 21:24) and the Gospel of Luke (Luke 1:1–4), both

of which have something to tell about the method employed in using the material at hand. We have to look elsewhere, therefore, for any information concerning the origin of Mark's Gospel except what may be obtained by comparing the writing with the other Gospels. The early commentators seem to have neglected this Gospel. Victor of Antioch (fifth or sixth century), the earliest known commentator on Mark, states that a number of expositors had treated the Gospels of Matthew and John and a few had dealt with Luke but that he had been unable to discover a single commentary upon Mark.

It is plain that for a long time Mark's Gospel was less esteemed and less used than the others, particularly less than the Gospels of Matthew and John, the work of apostles, while Mark's at best was only the work of an apostle's disciple. As compared with Luke's Gospel, it was much briefer and less complete and without Luke's literary charm. Besides, Irenaeus asserted that Mark's Gospel was later than that of Matthew and of less intrinsic historical worth. His order of the Gospels is: Matthew (in Aramaic first), Mark, Luke, John. Augustine speaks of Mark as the "follower and abbreviator of Matthew," a view that seems directly counter to the modern view. The uncertainty among the ancient writers as to the place and value of Mark's Gospel is shown by the fact that different writers used each of the symbols to describe Mark—the lion, the man, the ox, and the eagle. And yet the priority of Mark has been generally accepted by modern scholars.

3. *The True Origin of Mark's Gospel Preserved from the First.*—So, then, we moderns plume ourselves on a clearer conception of the critical and historical value of Mark's Gospel than many of the ancients. After all, however, the ancients seemed to have known the true origin of Mark's Gospel. Papias (quoted in Eusebius, H. E. iii, 39) gives a true

picture of the Gospel of Mark as we have it today. One could wish that Eusebius had given all that Papias had to say on the subject. Papias quotes the Presbyter John as the authority for his words about Mark's Gospel. This Presbyter John was almost certainly the apostle John. If so, we have here a criticism of the Second Gospel by the apostle John as reported by Papias. This criticism credits this Gospel with accuracy of statement but lack of order, although modern scholars consider Mark's Gospel as the framework of both Matthew and Luke. Probably by "order" here is meant fulness and completeness as compared with the other Gospels rather than mere chronology. This point is true, for Mark's Gospel has nothing about the infancy and youth of Jesus like Matthew and John, nothing about the early ministry of Jesus like John except the baptism and temptation of Jesus. It is mainly a narration of leading events in the Galilean ministry of Jesus with the story of Passion Week and the resurrection.

4. *Connection of Mark with Peter.*—The connection of Mark and Peter is attested by Irenaeus, Clement of Alexandria, Tertullian, Origen, Eusebius, Epiphanius, and Jerome. They do not agree in all details as to time and place of the writing of the Gospel, the occasion for Mark's doing it, or the extent of Peter's influence on the work. Rome is the place usually assigned, and the impulse is given to the Roman Christians who wished Mark to preserve for them the teachings of Peter about Christ. This was done with the silent acquiescence of Peter (Clement of Alexandria), with Peter's approval and authorization (Jerome), after Peter's death (Irenaeus). We may pass by the various discrepancies in the tradition with the recognition of the undoubted fact that Mark was associated with Peter in Rome (Babylon), according to Peter's own words (1 Pet. 5:13). Some have suggested that Peter refers to his purpose to see to the

preservation of his knowledge of Christ in his words in 2 Peter 1:15, assuming the genuineness of this disputed epistle.

It may be said at once that there is nothing in Mark's Gospel inconsistent with this tradition that Mark used Peter's recollections of Jesus in the preparation of his Gospel. We do not have to say that Mark had no other source of information or that he acted as the mere amanuensis of Peter who dictated the Gospel. Mark's mother, Mary, was a leader in the Jerusalem church, and her home was the resort of the great spirits in early Christianity (Acts 12:12). Peter, Barnabas, John, and the rest would here talk freely in conversation and sermons about Jesus' life and work. It is quite possible that John Mark early began to make notes of some of these things. At any rate, when Paul speaks of Mark as "useful to me for ministering" (2 Tim. 4:11) while with him in Rome (Col. 4:10), it may be that he has reference to Mark's reports of what Peter and the rest had said about Christ. Indeed, Mark's Gospel may already have been written before Paul was in Rome the first time. Paul may have read it and may even refer to this service of Mark. It is worthy of notice also that the report of Peter's sermon at Caesarea (Acts 10:36–43) is strangely like the general outlines of Mark's Gospel. Mark may even have been one of the six with Peter on this occasion and may have made fragmentary notes of this and of other discourses by Peter.

5. *Notes of an Eyewitness.*—The notes of an eyewitness are manifest in Mark's Gospel. They are admitted by all and include such details as the look of anger (3:5), the single pillow in the boat (4:38), the disposal of the five thousand like garden beds (6:40), the green grass (6:39), Christ sighing over the blindness of the Pharisees (8:12), taking the children in his arms (9:36, 10:16), Christ's look of love upon the rich young ruler (10:21), and the cloud upon the

21

young man's face (10:22). The graphic style of Mark is seen also in his frequent use of the imperfect tense to describe the scene, as the picture of Jesus watching the crowds and the rich in particular as they cast their gifts into the treasury (12:41). The historical present is also very common and is due to the same vividness and realistic imagination of an eyewitness. Mark sees the picture going on because of Peter's vivid description in his discourses. These picturesque details do not prove that Peter is responsible for them, but only that they are due to an eyewitness. The early writers, as we have seen, ascribe the body of the Gospel to Peter as the ultimate source. The character of the Gospel is in perfect harmony with this uniform tradition. The very unobtrusiveness of the Petrine touches increases their importance.

6. *The Sources of Mark's Gospel.*—We are confronted, therefore, with the sources of Mark's information. It is not necessary to assume that Peter was the sole source for Mark's Gospel. If Papias is correct in his statement that Mark was not a personal follower of Jesus and did not even hear him, he yet lived in Jerusalem and had access to the reports of many who did hear Jesus and who were eyewitnesses of the incidents in Christ's life. There is no more reason for confining Mark to one source than Luke. It is quite correct to insist that we must be willing to think of the "sources of sources." Mark's Gospel and Q (the Logia) themselves are based on sources. Luke fortunately has an historian's introduction to his Gospel and frankly records his method of investigation and use of materials for his book. He does not claim "originality." That is the very last qualification for the reliable historian. He must never invent his information. That he must obtain from others unless he is a participator in the events or a spectator of them.

When Luke wrote, many had undertaken "to draw up a narrative concerning these matters which have been fulfilled among us" (1:1). Luke is himself a Greek Christian of Asia Minor or of Macedonia and probably had no personal acquaintance with the great matters of the recent past connected with the life and work of Jesus. We know, however, that he spent two years in Palestine when Paul was a prisoner at Caesarea (24:27), assuming that Luke is the author of Acts. He had ample time and opportunity during this period to get firsthand information from those who were close to Christ while on earth. He may even have seen and conversed with Mary, the mother of Jesus, and his account of the birth of Jesus is certainly told from her standpoint, as that in Matthew is reported from the point of view of Joseph. At Caesarea resided Philip, deacon and evangelist, and his four daughters (Acts 21:8 f.). In Jerusalem Luke would see James the Lord's brother and many others, men and women who were full of the great deeds and words of Jesus. Luke distinctly states that he received help from those "who from the beginning were eyewitnesses and ministers of the word" and who were thus in full possession of the facts. He had and used oral testimony, therefore, beyond a doubt.

If Luke did so, why should not Mark have done likewise apart from Peter's oral witness, of which Mark probably made frequent notes? It is not necessary to go back to the oral theory as the explanation of all the similarities and differences in the Synoptic Gospels. The difficulty in the Synoptic problem has been precisely this, that men have tried to explain all the phenomena by one hypothesis instead of being willing to see all the facts and to allow the free play of life instead of the narrow vise of a hard and fast theory. It has been repeatedly shown that the evangelists are not mere copyists but historians. They are not slavishly transcribing minute details from this or that document or jotting down stenographic reports or discourses. They do use reliable sources of information, but they often retell the story in their own words or dovetail the language from one source into their narration with the freedom of ancient and modern historians. Variations of language are not matters for surprise but are to be expected.

And yet there is a sense in which the Gospels are not exactly histories. That is to say, they are not mere objective records which are colorless and noncommittal. They are all party pamphlets in the sense that they are written by men wholly committed to the acceptance of Jesus of Nazareth as the Jewish Messiah, but yet not such as the Pharisees expected. He is the real Messiah and King of the spiritual kingdom of God in the hearts of men and is both Son of God and Son of man. All four Gospels champion this thesis and prove it, though each has its own angle of vision.

The approach is individual in each instance, and the touch to the picture is different, though the broad outline is the same. Mark's Gospel is more objective but is still a theological interpretation of Jesus for the Roman world. Matthew's Gospel is a direct plea to Jewish readers to show that Jesus is the Jewish Messiah. Luke's Gospel has the broader outlook of the Greek culture and presents the universal aspects of Christ the Saviour of men. John's Gospel gives the eternal relations of Christ's person and work and interprets Christ's deity in terms of the current philosophy.

It is always important to insist that we take note of the actual conditions (psychological and external) under which the Gospels were written. The use of papyrus rolls instead of codices or printed books played its part in the matter of convenience in consulting the documents.

7. *Mark Used by Luke and Matthew.*—Luke states (1: 1–4) also that he made use of the written accounts of the life of Jesus. The ancients of the first century were great letter writers, as we know from the papyri. They used shorthand

and made notes of all sorts. Cicero employed shorthand in the trial of Catiline, and it was in common use in the first century A.D. We must get rid of the idea that the first century was an ignorant age. Mahaffy (*Progress of Hellenism,* p. 137) has shown that the Graeco-Roman civilization "was so perfect that, as far as it reached, men were more cultivated in the strict sense than they ever have been since." He adds, "The Hellenistic world was more cultivated in argument than we are nowadays."

Palestine was not in a backwater but right in the stream of Greek culture as it flowed north and south, east and west. The Pharisees resisted the influences of Hellenism, but it was pervasive nevertheless. This was a period of great literary activity in the Jewish world. This does not prove but certainly makes possible the theory that the non-Marcan materials (i.e., Q) were given written form during the public ministry of Jesus. If Matthew the publican, who was used to making and keeping data, wrote Q, he may very well have made copious notes of the sayings of Jesus which he so often heard. Luke expressly says that many undertook to draw up a narrative. The language implies an orderly arrangement of some sort of a more or less extended character. By Luke's time the matter had passed beyond the stage of notes or jottings or groups of incidents or anecdotes. Papyrus discoveries have restored some of the sayings of Jesus (Logia) introduced with the formula "Jesus says."

Luke throws no discredit on his sources or the use made of the data by previous narratives. He does affirm that, like a true historian in the spirit of a Thucydides, he has made accurate research through all the data at hand, both oral and written, and has endeavored to make an orderly presentation of the real facts in order that his friend and probable patron Theophilus may "know the certainty concerning the things wherein thou wast instructed" (1:4). He subjected tradition to the crucible of criticism as far as he was able to exercise it. We have already seen the probable judgment of the apostle John (as reported by Papias) concerning the value of Mark's Gospel. Then we have the probable reference of Luke to Mark's Gospel as one of the sources which he used in the construction of his book.

We may grant more literary skill to Luke than to Matthew and Mark, but there is no essential reason for doubting that they pursued approximately the same method as Luke in preparing the Gospels which we have. The sources probably varied, and we must allow full play for the individual judgment of the evangelist. There can be no rigid rule to which each writer must have conformed. We must allow room for the individual habits of each author. One would trust his memory over a longer period, while another might turn more quickly to written sources.

Did Luke, in fact, make use of Mark's Gospel? It is the general opinion of New Testament scholars and has been argued conclusively that Mark's Gospel is one of the main sources of our canonical Matthew and Luke. By many scholars it is no longer regarded as hypothesis but as established fact. That is perhaps too strongly put, in light of the fact that there are still those who hold to the priority of Matthew in an early Aramaic form. To be sure, Matthew could be prior to Mark and Mark still be prior to Luke. But as a rule, the scholars who make Mark prior to Luke also place it before Matthew.

The Two-Document Hypothesis lies at the basis of most of the progress made in our knowledge of the origin of the Synoptic Gospels. This position is accepted by Sanday and the other writers in the *Oxford Studies in the Synoptic Problem.* "We assume what is commonly known as the 'Two-Document Hypothesis.' We assume that the marked resemblances between the first Three Gospels are due to the use of common documents, and that the fundamental documents are two in number." These documents are our Mark or "a complete Gospel identical with our St. Mark's, which was used by the Evangelists whom we know as St. Matthew and St. Luke," and a collection consisting mainly of discourses "which supplied the groundwork of certain common matter in St. Matthew and St. Luke." It is not difficult for one to see the force of this statement of Sanday if he will look at the parallel tables of matter common to Mark, Matthew, and Luke in any harmony of the Gospels.

Thus one is bound to see that the same general order of events is followed and that the framework of Mark lies at the basis of both Matthew and Luke. Mark's order is confirmed either by Matthew or Luke, and the greater part of it by both. Luke is generally in fair agreement with Mark when the two are dealing with the same events. Out of 106 sections of Mark's Gospel only four, besides the headline, are absent from both Matthew and Luke. Ninety-three are in Matthew and eighty-one in Luke. There is a great deal of material in both Matthew and Luke which is not in Mark, while only one-sixth of Mark's Gospel occurs in it alone. And most of this peculiar Marcan material is due to greater fulness of detail in the picturesque presentation of the same events narrated in Matthew and Luke.

There are, however, some eighty verses in Mark that have no parallel in Matthew or Luke. It is far more likely that the brief and lifelike narration of Mark was amplified by Matthew and Luke than that Mark, as Augustine said, abbreviated Matthew or Luke. It can be shown that some documentary connection between the Synoptic Gospels is necessary by a case like that in Matthew 9:6, Mark 2:10, and Luke 5:24 when right in the midst of a saying of Jesus there is inserted in each instance a parenthetical comment of the writer: "Then saith he to the sick of the palsy." There are other instances as clear as this. The argument may therefore be considered as complete. Luke did make use of Mark, and so apparently did Matthew.

8. *Mark and Q.*—The purpose of this article does not call for an extensive discussion of Q, the other document apparently used in common by Matthew and Luke. Critics are not agreed as to the contents of the hypothetical Q. Some would confine it to the matter common to Matthew and Luke. Others would assign to Q much of the non-Marcan matter in either Matthew or Luke. Others still would make it identical with Papias' Logia of Matthew. But did Mark have the use of Q also? Streeter has a very able treatment of *St. Mark's Knowledge and Use of Q*. He argues that Mark knew and used Q from memory and wrote not to supersede Q but to supplement it, since Q consisted mainly of discourses, just as John wrote his Gospel to supplement the Synoptic Gospels. If this is true, the age of Q becomes a subject of deep interest.

It does not fall within the purpose of this article to discuss the origin of our canonical Matthew. My own views on that subject are given in the Introduction to my *Handbook to Matthew* in the "Bible for Homes and School" series. I do not feel that the case of Matthew is as clear as that of Luke who discusses his use of his sources. Papias' remark about the Aramaic Logia of Matthew is hard to set aside, and yet our present Matthew does not appear to be a translation of an Aramaic original. It is quite possible that Matthew did first prepare an Aramaic Logia and that he later wrote his expanded Gospel in Greek. This Aramaic Logia, translated into Greek, may be the Q used by Matthew and Luke and probably also by Mark.

We know that Luke used Aramaic sources (written or oral) for the first two chapters of his Gospel and probably also for the opening chapters of Acts. Mark makes some transliterations and then translations of Aramaic words used by Jesus, who certainly spoke much, possibly mainly, in Aramaic. But I must contend that Jesus spoke at times in the current Greek. It has been held by several scholars that Mark wrote originally in Aramaic. But it is difficult to think of our Greek Mark as a translation and, as Swete says, a translator would not have both transliterated and translated Aramaic words. Besides, Papias knew nothing of an Aramaic Mark. Still less is to be said for the idea of a Latin Mark. Greek was the language of culture in Rome itself, as we see from Paul's epistle to the Romans. The Latin terms in Mark's Gospel are chiefly political, military, or monetary, as is natural.

It remains for us to consider the possible revision of Mark's Gospel. Is our present Mark the original Mark? On this point Swete is clear and positive. "The present writer has risen from his study of the Gospel with a strong sense of the unity of the work, and can echo the *requiescat Ur-Markus* which ends a recent discussion. But he is not prepared to express an opinion as to the nature and extent of the editorial revision which St. Mark's original has undergone—a point which he desires to reserve for further consideration." This judgment probably represents the sanest criticism of the day.

There are some indications in our present Mark of editorial additions of a later date than the original work. The most important of these is, of course, the disputed ending after 16:8 which occurs in three forms. Some evidence exists also of the use of Matthew's Gospel by Mark as we now have it. This evidence is not conclusive in spite of the arguments which have been advanced. The priority of our Mark in these instances to Matthew and Luke is not certain. But editorial revision will account sufficiently for these few instances, if they are really later. Bacon is certain of this redactor and undertakes to point out the extent of his work. It is quite possible that a few additions were made to the original Mark by the author himself. For this reason Mark has been called "at once the oldest and the youngest of the Synoptics." There is no doubt at all that Mark used a variety of sources for his Gospel, as did Matthew and Luke. It is not possible and not necessary to decide every detail about his sources; one need not be so "overelaborate." There were, indeed, major sources and minor sources for each of the Synoptic Gospels.

If Mark used Q, this ancient document comes near the time of our Lord's ministry and death. We seem to be on terra firma in Synoptic criticism in spite of many complexities and perplexities. The historical worth of Mark and of Q is not to be lightly set aside. Criticism can claim that it has restored to modern scholars the historical character of the Synoptic Gospels as the result of a century of discussion. The modern man can employ with confidence the same intellectual tools here that he uses in his other studies. And in Mark and Q he is face to face with Jesus Christ in all his glorious humanity and his wondrous deity, Son of man and Son of God.

Peter's Influence on
Mark's Gospel

*They delivered them unto us, who from the be-
ginning were eyewitnesses and ministers of the
word.*   LUKE 1:2.

1. *Importance of the Subject.*—The influence of Peter
on Mark's Gospel is a matter of so much importance that it
calls for separate and detailed discussion in addition to the
various allusions already made to the subject. The modern
theories of the origin of Mark's Gospel all postulate the discourses of Simon Peter as the chief source. Even radical
critics have come to admit that Mark was in close touch
with Peter and the early Christian group. The tradition is
perfectly clear that this Gospel was written by John Mark
about 70. Only those who hold that the life of Jesus itself
does not belong to the realm of history but to the world of
myth have been willing to reject Marcan authorship or to
place its date impossibly late. But behind Mark stands the
figure of Simon Peter.

Von Soden boldly describes this Gospel as "the Reminiscences of St. Peter written by St. Mark," though he holds to
the redactor theory for our present Mark. Von Soden's estimate of Mark and Matthew is a good antidote for Schweitzer's pessimism: "Never has mankind listened to simpler,

more direct, more living, and more convincing narratives drawn from the life of one of the great ones of human history. Never has there been bestowed upon men a work of purer literary art—a work wherein the artist is more completely effaced by his subject—than in these two original Gospels."

2. *The Early Testimony.*—But why must we consider Peter the chief source of Mark's Gospel? The testimony of the early Christian writers is specific on this point. Papias is the first. He says, as quoted in Eusebius:

And this the Elder said: Mark, indeed, became Peter's interpreter and wrote accurately as many things as he remembered of the things said or done by Christ, not, however, in order. For neither did he hear the Lord nor did he follow at his side; but afterwards, as I said (he followed) Peter, who used to adapt his teachings to the needs (of his hearers), but not as though he were making a connected (or full) account of the Lord's discourses. So then Mark made no mistake in thus writing some things as he recalled them; for he took thought for one thing not to omit anything of what he heard nor to make any false statement therein.

We could sincerely wish that Papias had said more or that if he did, Eusebius had quoted all of it. Still, we do have quite a deal in this statement of Papias which belongs to the period 125–140. The Elder is here the Presbyter John, who has been identified with the apostle John. If the Elder here is the apostle John, then Papias records this estimate of Mark's writing, the recollections of Peter, from the apostle John himself. We have John's opinion of the worth of Peter's discourses about Jesus and of Mark's report of them. Here we touch Gospel criticism in its early stages, and it is a refreshing glimpse that we get of the whole subject. It is quite possible that the Fourth Gospel shows traces of the author's acquaintance with the Gospel of Mark. It is generally admitted that Luke used Mark as one of his sources and refers to him in his Gospel (1:1–4). If so, we have two references to Mark's work by writers of the Gospels (first in Luke and later in the quotation in Papias). Luke gives no details, but John does, as reported by Papias.

It is extremely interesting to examine carefully what John has to say about Mark's Gospel, since John wrote the Fourth Gospel with full knowledge of what Mark and the rest had written. We have, to be sure, only Papias' interpretation of the Elder's views about Mark, and the passage is quite condensed. But a number of points stand out clearly. It is not said that Mark's Gospel contains nothing except what Peter said. We are not to think of Peter dictating the Gospel to Mark who merely acted as Peter's amanuensis, as Tertius did for Paul's epistle to the Romans (16:22). Justin Martyr says that Jesus "imposed on one of the apostles the name Peter, and when this accorded in his 'Memoirs' with this other fact that he named the two sons of Zebedee 'Boanerges,' which means 'Sons of Thunder.'" Evidently Justin means to term Mark's Gospel "Peter's Memoirs," after the analogy of Xenophon's "Memorabilia of Socrates."

Origen also says, "The Second is that according to Mark who prepared it, as Peter guided him, who therefore, in his catholic epistle acknowledged the evangelist as his son." Origen not only held that Mark wrote his Gospel while Peter was alive and before the First Epistle of Peter was written, but under the immediate supervision of Peter, though not necessarily at his dictation. But Tertullian speaks of "that which was published by Mark, for it may be attributed to Peter, whose interpreter Mark was." Papias does call Mark Peter's interpreter or dragoman, but he does not say that Peter acted in that capacity in the writing of his Gospel. In fact, he really affirms that he did not do so, for the words "as many as he remembered" naturally mean that Mark wrote out his recollections after hearing Peter speak. It was not strictly shorthand copy, unless brief notes, but recollections after the discourse was over. The interval may have been very brief in most cases, as it probably was, writing thus some things as he recalled them.

Irenaeus seems to affirm that Peter and Paul were both dead when Mark wrote out his reminiscences of Peter's discourses about Jesus. "But, after the departure of these, Mark, the disciple and interpreter of Peter, even he has handed down to us the things that were preached by Peter." It has been argued by some that Peter had in mind Mark's Gospel in 2 Peter 1:15: "Yea, I will give diligence that at every time ye may be able after my decease to call these things to remembrance." It is interesting to note also that Peter calls himself and others "eyewitnesses" of the majesty of Jesus on the Mount of Transfiguration, just as Luke spoke of consulting "eyewitnesses" for his Gospel (1:2).

Clement of Alexandria takes the view that Peter knew of Mark's purpose to write his Gospel at the suggestion of the Roman Christians: "When Peter learned it, he neither eagerly hindered nor approved it." But Jerome says, "When Peter heard of it, he gave his approval and authorized it to be read in the churches." Jerome actually says, "As the blessed Peter had Mark whose Gospel was prepared, Peter narrating and Mark writing." One can but feel that the tradition about Peter's connection with Mark's Gospel has thus grown through the centuries since the simple statement of Papias.

Eusebius, who preserves Papias' words for us, has this addition: "When the apostle knew, by revelation of the Spirit, what was done, he was pleased with the eagerness of the men and authorized the writing to be read in the churches." Eusebius also has this: "Though Peter did not undertake,

34

through excess of diffidence, to write a Gospel, yet it was all along commonly said that Mark, who had become his intimate acquaintance and companion, made memoirs of the discourses of Peter concerning the deeds of Jesus." The conclusion of Eusebius is, therefore: "Mark, indeed, writes this; but it is Peter who so witnesses about himself, for all that is in Mark are memoirs of the discourses of Peter." Here, then, Eusebius attributes the whole of Mark's Gospel to Peter. Papias does not say this and, in fact, rather implies the contrary, though clearly making Peter's discourses the main source of the Second Gospel. Modern criticism here agrees with Papias rather than with Eusebius and Jerome.

Mark almost certainly had other sources of information. Papias does not say whether Peter was alive or not when Mark wrote his recollection of the discourses. There is no inherent probability against the position that Peter was alive. He may even have seen Mark's Gospel and have approved it, but he did not dictate it. This is clear from modern study. Mark is wholly responsible for what he put into the book. He acted as a real author and composed the Gospel with the best sources at his disposal, relying chiefly on Peter's sermons. The apostle John and Papias commend him for so doing. In a true sense, therefore, the Second Gospel is Peter's memorabilia of Jesus, but Mark is responsible for the literary aspects of the book.

3. *Mark's Gospel More than a Collection of Discourses.*—Papias makes clear that Mark's Gospel is more than a collection of discourses. It is true that Papias speaks of "the Lord's discourses," saying that this is the probable meaning here of Logia, though the word is applied to narrative as well as sayings. It is "a little word," a brief oracle, therefore, any utterance without regard to its length. In the New Testament the word is applied also to the contents of the Mosaic law (Acts 7:38), and then to the substance of the

Christian religion (Heb. 5:12). But it is evident that Mark, according to Papias, did more than write down the sayings of Jesus, for he describes this Gospel as containing "the things said or done by Christ." Peter discussed in his discourses both the deeds and the words of Jesus, as we see from Acts 10:34–41.

When we turn to the Gospel of Mark, we find in it more of the deeds than the sayings of Christ, and it is in Matthew, Luke, and John that we find more of the discourses of Christ. The modern theory is that the Logia of Jesus, representing a collection of Christ's sayings and possibly made by Matthew himself, is used along with Mark as the two main sources of Matthew and Luke. Mark gives the narrative and Q (the Logia) the discourses. But Mark is not without sayings of Christ, including some parables and the eschatological discourse in chapter 13 (the so-called "little apocalypse"). There is nothing in our canonical Mark that makes it more unlikely that Papias' description applies to it. We do not need to picture an Ur-Marcus for Papias.

4. *Mark's Use of His Material.*—Papias quotes the Elder as saying that Mark wrote "not in order" and "not as if he were making a connected arrangement of the Lord's discourses." But modern criticism finds the order of Mark preserved almost exactly in Luke and in its broad features in Matthew, who is topical in certain portions of his Gospel. Luke claims to write "in order" (1:3), and Luke's order is that of Mark. It is likely, however, that Papias does not mean quite the same by "order" that Luke does. Luke has endeavored to produce a fairly complete and systematic presentation of his material in chronological order in the main. Mark, according to Papias, is a rather incomplete setting forth of certain aspects of Christ's life derived chiefly from Peter's discourses about Jesus. Now, as a matter of fact, Mark's Gospel has nothing about the infancy and the early

life of Jesus as we have in Matthew and in Luke, and nothing concerning the early ministry as we find in John. It is, after the baptism of Jesus by John, mainly a sketch of the Galilean ministry with some incidents of the last year away from Galilee and the picture of Passion Week.

This is in perfect harmony with the sketch of Peter's preaching in Acts 10:34–41 but is also in accord with the description of Papias, who insists that Mark wrote "accurately," just as Luke claimed for his work (1:3). Indeed, Papias insists, on the authority of the Elder, that Mark's one concern was to make no mistake, either by omission of what he knew or by false statement. Here again Mark is justified in modern criticism, which bears witness to the skill and accuracy of his work. First place in historical value is accorded Mark's Gospel because it ranks first in order of time and is incorporated almost bodily into Matthew and Luke. This is not to discredit Matthew and Luke but simply to say that in Mark we possess the chief source used by both of them.

Papias does not say that Mark reproduced everything that Peter said. It was not a mechanical performance on Mark's part, but he did his work, "writing thus some things as he recalled them." The use of "some" implies that he made a selection out of the numerous discourses of Peter, of which he may have made notes, but took pains not to pass anything by that was really important and, in particular, not to tell an untruth. This is a pleasing word for any historian's work. Mark did not give way to fancy or to legend, of which we see a riot in the apocryphal gospels. He did not invent incidents to embellish his narrative or to enhance the power and glory of Jesus. He did not make up discourses for Jesus as Thucydides did for his heroes. Mark indulged in no eulogy of Jesus. He told in straightforward manner the simple, unvarnished story of the facts as he had heard Peter do. The facts and words of Jesus are more eloquent than any adjectives that can be applied to them. They speak for themselves.

Matthew and Luke follow Mark in their wondrous restraint in picturing Jesus. This characteristic simplicity is the very highest art, which partly explains how these Gospels rank as the greatest literary productions of the ages through sheer reality. There is the utter absence of anything artificial or dramatic, though the action itself is overwhelming. It is the greatest story of the ages told in the current vernacular Greek by unsophisticated men who had no literary aspirations. They have excelled all other writers because they have seen Jesus only and have been willing to let the words and deeds of Christ speak for themselves. Thus the very absence of artifice has become consummate and unapproachable art. To be sure, they had the supreme subject, but so had the apocryphal gospels with their silly stories and legends. The difference lies in the element of reality and truth.

The Gospels surpass all other books because the words of Jesus are the most original and vital of all time and because his life is the highest conception of God that the world knows. The Gospels in utter childlike simplicity succeed in taking Jesus as he is and letting us see him. They do it each in his own way, but they all do this supreme thing. Forever we must therefore come back to the Gospels for our picture of Christ. At bottom the picture comes from Peter in the Synoptic Gospels and John in the Fourth Gospel.

5. *Peter's Eyes.*—In Mark's Gospel we catch the first draft of the portrait. Mark has been willing and able to use Peter's eyes for us. He has left the little turns of speech that Peter used to give color to his discourses. So in Mark we *see* Jesus with more distinctness of outline than in any of the Gospels. We see him at work, almost hear his voice. If one looks at his harmony of the Gospels, he will see that many of

the vivid touches in Matthew and Luke really come from Mark, though they do omit many that are in the original passage in Mark. Mark's love of the historical present is largely dropped in Matthew and Luke. Mark is more fond of the imperfect tense than any of the other Gospel writers. Here again he is probably seeing through the eyes of Peter, who thus pictured the scene for his hearers. We see the same vividness in Mark's constant use of "straightway." It is all action and movement like real life.

It is clear that in Mark's Gospel we have reports that come from an eyewitness. This can be shown abundantly in the many little details that occur in Mark's Gospel alone. His Gospel is the briefest of all, and yet it is often fullest when he does give an incident because he supplies so many little items that fill out the picture. Most of them are the things that an alert mind like that of Peter would notice. It will be interesting to note some of them, though by no means all.

In Mark 1:29–37 we have an incident that is obviously Petrine. After preaching in the synagogue in Capernaum, Jesus went with James and John to "the house of Simon and Andrew." Mark alone has "and Andrew." Evidently Andrew, probably a bachelor, lived with his brother Peter's family. Peter delicately includes Andrew as copartner in the house. But Jesus is here for dinner, like our Sunday dinner after church, and Peter's mother-in-law is ill of fever, probably a sudden attack. "And straightway they tell him of her," Mark notes with his love for the historical present and with the vivid narrative of Peter in his mind. Mark drops back into the past tense but preserves the picturesque details which he remembers from Peter's story: "He came and took her by the hand, and raised her up," just like the loving physician that Jesus was. We see Jesus standing by the bedside and tenderly taking the hand of the sick woman.

That evening when the sun set, Mark says that a great crowd of sick folk came. They had heard of the healing of the demoniac in the synagogue that morning, and then of the cure of Peter's mother-in-law. So here they come with all sorts of diseases. "And all the city was gathered together at the door," Mark says. Probably Jesus stood in the door and healed them as they passed by, a wondering throng. It was Peter's door, and he probably stood proudly near Jesus as he healed the moving procession. It is easy to see why Peter should have mentioned the door.

Next morning, "a great while before day," Mark says, Jesus rose up and went out from Peter's house, probably not without Peter's observing it and wondering about it. Jesus went to "a desert place, and there prayed." The imperfect tense is used to indicate that Jesus continued in prayer a long time, kept on praying, was still praying when Peter "found him." For Peter had the crowds on his hands when day came and did not know what to do with them. Not yet had Peter begun to heal the sick. So "Simon and they that were with him followed after him" until they found him. Peter led a search party for Jesus in the early dawn and found him at prayer. Mark uses a very striking word for "followed after." It means pursue, to rush down upon as in a chase for game. Paul uses the simple verb twice of Christ as his goal (Phil. 3:12, 14). Probably Peter in telling the incident said, "We rushed out of the house after Jesus," unless he told it in Aramaic. If so, then this is Mark's translation of Peter's vivid description. Mark feels the touch of life in his style and goes on with the historical present: "And say unto him, All are seeking thee" (preserving here Peter's own words in the direct discourse).

Not all the incidents in Mark's Gospel are as closely linked with Peter's own life as the one above, but many others reveal the same traits of the eyewitness who is telling what he has seen with his own eyes. The healing of the paralytic let down through the roof is a case in point (2:1–12). Mark says, "It was noised that he was in the house," possibly Peter's house again. At any rate, we catch Peter's quick eyes in the narrative of Mark. The crowd was so great "that there was no longer room for them, no, not even about the door." The other time the crowd passed on by the door, but here they stood and listened to Jesus and blocked the door. Besides, that was a local crowd from Capernaum, while this crowd came "out of every village of Galilee and Judea and Jerusalem" (Luke 5:17). Through this press and jam "they come [historical present again], bringing unto him a man sick of the palsy, borne of four" (alone in Mark). All this Peter's eye took in. What were the men to do? "They could not come nigh unto him for the crowd." They evidently climbed up the outside stairway to the flat roof, carrying the man as they went. Then "they uncovered the roof where he was," right over Jesus. "And when they had broken it up [dug up the tiles], they let down the bed whereon the sick of the palsy lay."

It was a dramatic moment, and the courage and faith of these four men at once caught the attention of Jesus, who turned and said, "Son, thy sins are forgiven." This Jesus said without healing the palsied man. Perhaps his palsy was due to sin on the man's part. But Jesus' claim of power to forgive sins, as if he were God, gave the Pharisees present a jolt. Mark says, "But there were certain of the scribes sitting there," in a bunch, off to one side. Peter noticed them and the quick interchange of glances between them at this "blasphemous" claim of Jesus. They "reasoned within themselves," but Jesus read their hearts. Peter and all of them felt the tenseness of the situation. It was electric, and Peter never forgot it.

Jesus, "perceiving in his spirit," Mark says, that the Pharisees were thus reasoning about him, proceeded to heal the man to prove the truth of his claim to power to forgive sins: "But that ye may know that the Son of man hath authority on earth to forgive sins (he saith to the sick of the palsy), I say unto thee, Arise, take up thy bed, and go unto thy house." The parenthesis is in a curious place, right in the middle of the sentence, and occurs in the same place in Matthew and Luke, obviously taken from Mark. But why did Mark put it there? Probably Peter did it in his preaching. "He says to the sick of the palsy" is something like our "says he," which in conversation is thrown in almost anywhere. The man got up and "went forth before them all." The crowd in amazement glorified God: "We never saw it on this fashion." It is hardly possible to find a livelier picture than Mark has here drawn.

So we might go on, if we had space and time, to other scenes in Mark's Gospel. In Capernaum, "when he was in the house" (Mark 9:33) again, probably Peter's house still, Jesus took a little child and "set him in the midst . . . taking him in his arms" (9:36). Tradition has it that it was Peter's own child who was thus used to rebuke the jealousy of the twelve. One is tempted to linger over many like details in Mark's Gospel that reveal the eye of Peter, like the deep sigh of Jesus (8:12), the look of love cast upon the rich young ruler (10:21), the indignation of Christ (10: 14), the amazement and fear of the disciples at the expression of Jesus (10:33), the sudden spring of Bartimeus as he flung away his garment and followed Jesus (10:50), seeing the fig tree afar off (11:13), Peter's recalling the incident the next day (11:21).

We see, then, that there is ample reason for the sober conclusion of modern scholarship that in Mark's Gospel we are dealing primarily with Peter's interpretation of Christ after his reception of the Holy Spirit at Pentecost. It is the enlightened and understanding Peter whom Mark reports and whose message is thus passed on to all the ages. It is quite possible that Mark made notes of Peter's preaching from time to time, beginning at an early date, using this and other data for the final book which we possess. The proof for the influence of Peter on Mark's Gospel rests on good evidence and is amply confirmed by the phenomena in the Gospel itself.

V

The Miraculous Element
in Mark's Gospel

*And at even, when the sun did set, they brought
unto him all that were sick, and them that were
possessed with demons. And all the city was gathered together at the door.* MARK 1:32–33.

1. *The Miraculous Still in Mark.*—For a while Mark's
Gospel had quite a vogue with certain critics who hoped by
means of it to get rid of the Johannine Christ and the
Pauline Christ. In Mark we have the "historical Jesus" instead of the "theological Christ." But the issue is now seen
to be quite otherwise. Pfleiderer (*Christian Origins*, p.
219) confesses it:

On the other hand, it must not be overlooked that even this
oldest Gospel-writer is guided by a decided apologetic purpose
in the selection and manipulation of his material. He wrote for
Heathen-Christians and wished to awaken or confirm the conviction that despite the rejection by the Jews, Jesus of Nazareth was
proven to be the Christ and the Son of God by wonders and
signs of every kind, especially by the wonders of baptism, transfiguration, and resurrection, that his victorious struggle against
the Jewish priestly and liturgical service erected a new Temple
beyond the senses in the congregation of Christ-believers in the
place of the old one of the senses, and that by the blood which he

44

had shed for many, he established a new covenant to take the place of the old covenant of the law.

Here Pfleiderer has correctly presented the purpose and method of Mark's Gospel, though he himself has no sympathy with that purpose. He notes that Mark is free from the stories of the birth of Jesus found in Matthew and Luke, "religious legends of no historical value," but even Mark gives "the miraculous event of the messianic sanctification of Jesus by a celestial voice and the descent of the Spirit in the shape of a dove," which "is self-evidently not history, but legend."

2. *Jesus Himself the Chief Miracle.*—It is clear, therefore, that we have not reached solid ground with critics like Pfleiderer when we get back of John and Paul, back of Luke and Matthew, to Mark and Q (the Logia of Jesus). These earliest sources of our knowledge of Jesus are vitiated for them by the presence of the miraculous element in the life of Jesus. The only way to get at the facts about Jesus, according to the liberal critics, is to drop all the supernatural and the miraculous and to construct our picture of Jesus out of the remnant. The deity of Christ was curtly dismissed by the liberals. Since he was man, a union with God in one person was impossible. The Synoptic investigation of the liberals was directed entirely toward the rediscovery of the earthly Jesus, the human being. It was held that Jesus never transcends the purely human and never presents himself as the object of faith. The major complaint against the liberal Christology is that it presents a picture of Jesus which at no time transcends the limits of the human and yet it claims for this conception of the "ideal man" the extremes of religious value and sets him up as an object of religious worship. It rejects the miraculous Christ and yet claims for him a unique position in the realm of humanity.

The first and foremost miraculous element in the Gospel of Mark is Jesus himself. The very headline of the Gospel is, "The beginning of the gospel of Jesus Christ, the Son of God" (1:1). Some manuscripts omit "the Son of God," but it is quite evident that this Gospel means to prove Jesus to be the Son of God as truly as the Fourth Gospel does. Jesus is received thus and makes this claim. There can be no real question about the supernatural claims of Jesus of Nazareth.

This supernatural Christ is in Mark's Gospel. The Spirit comes upon him as a dove at his baptism (1:10), the Father addresses him as his Son (1:11), the angels minister to him in his temptation (1:13), he is transfigured on the mountain and talks with Moses and Elijah, and the Father again addresses him as his Son (9:2–7), he affirms to the high priest that he is the Son of the Blessed (14:61 f.), he rises from the grave in proof of his claims to be the Son of God (16:6), and in the disputed close of the Gospel (16: 9–20) there is additional proof of Christ's resurrection and ascension.

The miracles wrought by Jesus come in this atmosphere and have to be considered as natural expressions of the divine energy possessed by Jesus. It is idle to strip away the miracles and retain the teachings. The two are so interwoven in Mark's Gospel that nothing of real value would remain. We have to face, therefore, in this earliest of our Gospels precisely the same problem that confronts us in John's Gospel, the credibility of the narratives with the miraculous element in them. It will not do to say that the age was credulous and that men were predisposed to accept Jesus as divine. The Gospels themselves reveal precisely the opposite situation. Jesus wrought miracles and taught in the midst of a keenly critical atmosphere with all the ecclesiastical leaders hostile to him and with his own disciples utterly unable to grasp the spiritual aspect of his mission and the promise of his own resurrection. They were so skeptical on this point that it required repeated manifestations to convince them of the reality of his resurrection. This is the great miracle of the Gospels, then—Jesus himself. Once credit the fact of his deity, the rest follows naturally. And there is no other way to take Mark's Gospel.

3. *Evolution and Miracle.*—It comes back at last to our idea of God. There is a sense in which we cannot conceive of a real, living God without a belief in miracles. We may think of an absentee God, or of a pantheistic universe, but not of a personal God who reigns in his world. The scientific objection to miracle has lost much of its force. The world is now seen to be not static but in a constant state of change. Theistic evolution is now more favorable to the belief in miracles. The world is not a finished machine but a growing organism.

One may or may not accept the theory of theistic evolution. Atheistic evolution, of course, denies the existence of God and tries to explain everything in terms of materialism. But few modern scientists go to that extreme. Matthew Arnold's dictum that miracles do not happen fails to satisfy modern scientists, who find that life transcends while combining with and controlling physical forces. The basic controversy in this area rests upon two distinct conceptions of the universe. One is that of a material universe absolutely sufficient in itself and completely furnished for its origination and career. The other is that of a physical universe, open to and dominated by a spiritual universe. We must make our choice, therefore, between these two conceptions before we come to the study of Mark's Gospel. No one today talks about violation of the laws of nature by miracle. We ourselves overcome the law of gravity by climbing and by flying in the air, but the law of gravity operates all the time. We overcome it by force. Surely God has his own per-

sonal will at all times and is himself superior to all the laws
that he has laid down for his universe.

4. *The Number of the Miracles in Mark.*—Without further
apology, therefore, we can come to Mark's Gospel and note
the miracles wrought by Jesus. They are usually given as
eighteen, but it all depends on what we consider a miracle.
We note the demoniac in the synagogue in Capernaum
(1:23–27), Peter's mother-in-law (1:30), the leper (1:40–
45), the paralytic (2:1–12), the man with a withered hand
(3:1–6), stilling the tempest (4:35–41), the Gadarene demoniac (5:1–20), the woman with an issue of blood (5:25–
34), raising of Jairus' daughter (5:21–24, 35–43), feeding the
five thousand (6:31–44), walking on the sea (6:45–52), the
daughter of the Syrophenician woman (7:24–30), the deaf
and dumb man (7:31–37), feeding the four thousand
(8:1–9), the blind man at Bethsaida-Julias (8:22–26), the
deaf and dumb demoniac and epileptic (9:14–29), blind
Bartimeus (10:46–52), the withering of the fig tree (11:12–
14, 20–25), and the cleansing of the Temple (11:15–18).
There are nineteen in this list, which counts the cleansing of
the Temple as a miracle. Leaving that out, there are eighteen.

But this list is by no means complete, for in Mark we have
a number of general descriptions of a great many miracles
wrought by Jesus. There is absolutely no means of telling
how many miracles were performed by Jesus. There were
probably many thousands. "And he healed many that were
sick with divers diseases, and cast out many demons" (1:34).
"And he went into their synagogues throughout all Galilee,
preaching and casting out demons" (1:39). "Lest they
should throng him: for he had healed many; insomuch that
as many as had plagues pressed upon him that they might
touch him" (3:9 f.). "And the scribes that came down
from Jerusalem said, He hath Beelzebub, and, By the prince

of the demons casteth he out the demons" (3:22). "And he could there do no mighty work, save that he laid his hands upon a few sick folk, and healed them" (6:5). "And ran round about that whole region, and began to carry about on their beds those that were sick, where they heard he was. And wheresoever he entered, into villages, or into cities, or into the country, they laid the sick in the marketplaces, and besought him that they might touch if it were but the border of his garment: and as many as touched were made whole" (6:55 f.).

One has only to let his imagination work a little to see the vast scale of this work of healing on the part of Jesus. One may note in passing also the work done by the apostles on this tour of Galilee: "And they cast out many demons, and anointed with oil many that were sick, and healed them" (6:13). If one will take out of Mark's Gospel all the miracles wrought by Jesus and every mention of the miraculous or the supernatural, he will have only a mutilated fragment. When the miraculous is removed, only a bare skeleton remains. In most of the reports action and authentic word are so closely interwoven that it is impossible to separate them. It is clear, therefore, that in Mark's Gospel, as in John's (20:30 f.), a selection has been made of representative miracles without any idea of exhaustiveness.

5. *Kinds of Miracles.*—Christ's miracles are most commonly divided into those performed on nature, on man, and on the spirit world. But there is no sharp line of cleavage. "Nature" with Christ covers all realms. He is at home everywhere. Human nature is a part of nature. The spirit world is also a part of God's world. Jesus is as much at home in his mastery of wind and wave as in healing a blind man. He expels the demons with the same ease with which he makes the loaves and fishes multiply for the five thousand and then for the four thousand. He walks on the sea and

withers the fig tree at a word. He raises the dead and attacks with uniform success all sorts of diseases. We do not get far in understanding Christ's power by any analysis of the kind of miracles wrought. Some were miracles of creative power, some of Providence. Some were miracles of personal faith, some of intercession, and some of compassion, such as healing on the sabbath day and raising the dead.

It is easier for modern men to understand some of Christ's cures than others. The cases of nervous disorder are now better understood because we know more about the influence of the mind on the body than we once did. But if these cures seem to us more credible than was once the case, we are not logically justified in repudiating the rest, as Harnack does, who will not believe that "a storm sea was stilled by a word." Rather, we should be constrained to believe what we cannot explain, since so much has become plainer. We must constantly keep in mind that God has laws unknown to us. They operate regardless of our ignorance of them. For instance, electricity, the atom, radium, and other discoveries are revolutionary to us.

6. *Miracle and Fact.*—We must always remember that the miracles of Jesus did not seem miraculous or unusual to him. The most real thing in his earthly life was his fellowship with his Father. The Fourth Gospel makes this perfectly plain (cf. John 5), but it comes out in Mark's Gospel also (1:1, 35; 9:7; 13:32). Jesus is here seen as a citizen of two worlds. He is the Son of man and the Son of God. He approaches human sin and sickness with the heart of the beloved physician that he is, but with the skill and power of the Father whose Son he is. He is thus able to make an unerring diagnosis and to touch the springs of life to drive away the germs of disease. We are fearfully and wonderfully made, and Jesus releases in men the forces of life that win the victory in the wonderful fight going on in all of us

50

for life or death. The miracles of Jesus are consonant with his loving heart of pity and tenderness. "If it be a revelation of grace, the miracles also must be gracious."

So then we must not draw a line between miracle and fact. A hundred years ago the airplane would have seemed a miracle. A railroad train in Gaul would have frightened Julius Caesar and his legions. "A miracle is on one side of it not a fact of this world, but of the invisible world." But it becomes a part of this world when it has taken place. A fact is a fact whether we comprehend it or not. It is sometimes argued that miracles can be dismissed because they cannot be proved to have happened exactly as recorded. But men do the most astounding things. An engineer proved conclusively that a steamship could never cross the Atlantic Ocean because it could not carry coal enough to get across. But the steamship went on across all the same. Nothing is impossible with God, nothing that is worthwhile, that is good, that appeals to God's heart. He has the power to do what he wills to do. That is the end of the whole matter.

7. *The Key to Miracle.*—Many who assume that miracles were really performed by Christ hold that the major problem today is the correlation of the ideas of the twentieth century with those of the first. This is undoubtedly true, and we should seek to bring historically verified facts into harmony with a reasonably interpreted philosophy of nature. But we maintain that the credibility of the miracles of Jesus does not depend upon our being able to square them with the current philsosphy of nature which we may hold, a constantly changing theory. In spite of our inability to comprehend all that is involved in the miraculous, we must agree that the key to miracles lies in the personality of God. If there are latent possibilities in man, who can say what God can or cannot do? If Christ is both God and man, we cannot properly deny to him the power of God.

51

8. *A Nonmiraculous Gospel.*—The miracles of Jesus will continue to be attacked, but there are modern defenders who know how to interpret modern thought in harmony with the law and will of God. It is true that today more emphasis is laid upon the spiritual and ethical content of the Gospels than upon the miracles and the supernatural attestation of the message. But it is not true that we can give up the miraculous element in Mark or any of the Gospels and have anything left that is worthwhile. We should have mere scraps of narrative with disjointed sayings and a purely human Jesus who was one of the most mistaken of men; a teacher full of hallucinations about himself; a miracle-monger like Simon Magus, not the wonder-worker of Mark's Gospel; a disappointed and misguided leader of a forlorn hope, not the Saviour of the world who gave his life a ransom for many (Mark 10:45); a teacher out of touch with modern life, not the star of hope for a sin-stricken race.

9. *The Renaissance of Wonder.*—The day has passed when serious scholars make scoff at wonder. Modern science has taught us much of the marvels of nature. Three Greek words are used in the Gospels to describe the works of Jesus—wonders, powers, and signs—all used together in Acts 2:22. The word for wonder occurs in Mark only in 13:22 and in connection with the signs wrought by false prophets who seek to lead astray the very elect. But the idea of wonder runs all through the Gospel of Mark. It takes all of these words to convey the full conception of a miracle of Jesus as a cause for wonder, as a work wrought by divine power, and as a sign of the truth of Christ's claim to be the Messiah, the Son of God.

Mere wonder does not take us very far if it stops there, but we do not make much headway in any direction without it. The child is constantly learning and greets the new knowledge of each day with open-eyed astonishment and delight.

The first miracle pictured in Mark 1:21–28 occurs in the synagogue at Capernaum. There the people "were astonished at his teaching," at the force and authority of it—"for he taught them as having authority and not as the scribes"— and at the novelty of it. "What is this? A new teaching!" But the biggest sensation on that day was that the unclean spirit went out of a man at the command of Jesus. As a result, "the report of him went out straightway everywhere into all the region of Galilee round about." It requires very little imagination to see how excitement spread into every direction as the outcome of this day's work. Something happened that day "at church" quite out of the ordinary.

Amazement in the synagogue is followed by the healing of Peter's mother-in-law (1:29–31). The two miracles are the occasion of a wonderful sunset scene at the door of the dwelling that very evening (1:32–34). Mark's language is picturesque, probably as Peter told it in his preaching. "At even, when the sun did set [possibly a glorious sunset] . . . all the city was gathered together at the door" (right in front of the door). Jesus apparently stood in the doorway and healed the passing crowds of sick folks and hushed the turbulent demoniacs. It was the hour of hope for all the stricken while the Great Physician was on hand. It is easy to see the stir in Capernaum at the close of this memorable sabbath day there, the first of many like it. There Jesus stood with no hospital, no medicine, no surgical instruments, but with power to give life.

But the excitement was too great and the strain was severe on Jesus (1:35). Our Lord felt the need of his Father's help and spent much of the night in prayer. What a reproach to us all in our self-complacent and easygoing way of doing Christian work! Peter probably told this also, for Mark's record is that "Simon and they that were with him followed after" Jesus in hot haste with the cry, "All are seeking thee."

So Jesus "went into their synagogues throughout all Galilee, preaching and casting out demons" (1:39). We can never quite comprehend the glory of this first dawn of Christ's power in Galilee. He healed a leper (1:40–45) and strictly charged him, "See thou say nothing to any man." But man-like, "he went out, and began to publish it much, and to spread abroad the matter, insomuch that Jesus could no more openly enter into a city, but was without in desert places," seeking to hide from the excitable populace. But Mark naively adds, "And they came to him from every quarter." Those were great days on earth.

One day Jesus was back in Capernaum and "it was noised that he was in the house" (or at home). That news was enough for the crowd which was soon so great "that there was no longer room for them, no, not even about the door" (2:2). Thus Mark introduces us to his description of the healing of the paralytic let down through the tile roof which was dug up (2:1–12). It is a graphic story. Jesus defied the Pharisees and healed the man to prove that he had power on earth to forgive sins and therefore was God himself. The man "arose, and straightway took up the bed, and went forth before them all," Mark says with characteristic love of detail, "insomuch that they were all amazed, and glorified God, saying, We never saw it on this fashion." They could not get used to the wonder of Christ in the presence of sin and sickness and sorrow.

The anger of the Pharisees takes a practical turn when the man with the withered hand is healed right before their very eyes in the synagogue and on the sabbath day (3:1–6). "They watched him," for the Pharisees had now come to expect that Jesus could do his miracles of healing when he wished and in defiance of their customs. They wished a further charge against him. Jesus was deliberate enough and "looked round about on them with anger." The holy anger of

Christ clashed with the murderous wrath of the Pharisees, who "went out, and straightway . . . took counsel against him, how they might destroy him."

The fame of Jesus drew "a great multitude from Galilee," and "from Judea, and from Jerusalem, and from Idumea, and beyond the Jordan, and about Tyre and Sidon" who came "hearing what great things he did" (3:7–12). The crowd pressed upon him so that he had a little boat to wait on him by the sea for escape. The people were eager to touch him and be healed as they passed. The demoniacs continued to hail Jesus as the Son of God.

Two explanations of Christ's power are given by Mark: one by his friends that "he is beside himself" (3:20 f.), probably including his mother and brothers (3:31–35), for the moment even Mary not understanding his conduct; the other by his enemies, the Pharisees, who said that Jesus cast out demons by Beelzebub (3:22–30). But both classes admit the reality of his cures. The extraordinary man is often accused of being peculiar.

Quite in contrast with this turbulent atmosphere is the picture of Jesus asleep in the boat with his head on the cushions, while the disciples are frightened to death by the fierceness of the storm. They have the Lord of nature with them in the boat and yet fear that all are sinking. When Christ shows that he is Master of wind and waves, they fear exceedingly. Even the apostles are not used to the many-sided man of Galilee whom they follow.

The scene changes quickly in Mark like a kaleidoscopic panorama. The wild man at Khersa (5:1–20) is one of the weirdest in history. Huxley ridiculed it as "the Gadarene pig affair."

There are difficulties in the narrative as to the loss of property and demons in hogs, but we are concerned here only with the tremendous effect of the cure of this terrible man of the tombs and mountains. The terror of the keepers of the swine when they saw the herd of hogs rush down headlong into the sea and drown was communicated to the neighbors who "began to beseech" Jesus "to depart from their borders." Jesus did depart, as he has probably done since, from many another region to its ruin. But "all men marvelled" at the story of the now calm and rational ex-demoniac.

The nervous strain on Jesus is shown by the case of the woman with an issue of blood (5:25–34). "And straightway Jesus, perceiving in himself that the power proceeding from him had gone forth, turned him about in the crowd, and said, "Who touched my garments?" There is the touch of nature that makes the whole world kin. What teacher or preacher has not felt power go out of him? It has gone out if the hearer has gotten any blessing. This "gone" feeling explains "blue Mondays" and lack of "liberty," as the old preachers used to say. Yes, and one can do no more until he has a fresh supply of divine energy. Even Jesus felt the strain of the work of healing and preaching. But he was not too worn to soothe and to bless this fearing and trembling woman.

The raising of Jairus' young daughter (5:35–43) made a profound impression. "They laughed him to scorn" when Jesus went on up to the room to restore her. Here at least was a point where the power of Jesus stopped. So the crowd argued he might keep men from dying, he could not bring back the dead. But all the same, Jesus drove death away. "And they were amazed straightway with a great amazement."

And yet there was a limit to the power of Christ. It was unbelief, and Jesus met this obstacle at Nazareth (6:1–6). "He marvelled because of their unbelief." What a commentary on the community in Nazareth where Jesus had spent his youth. "And he could there do no mighty work, save that he laid his hands upon a few sick folk, and healed them." Perhaps here we see the explanation of many a failure in church work today.

The third formal campaign through Galilee made a great impression, and even Herod Antipas at Tiberias was stirred intensely by it. He saw in Christ the ghost of John the Baptist whom he had beheaded (6:14–29). This guilty conscience haunted him, as is often the case when the Spirit of God does mighty works among men. Men's hearts are then searched to the depths.

Twice Christ fed the crowds east of the Sea of Galilee. Once it was near Bethsaida-Julias (6:30–44) and in Decapolis (8:1–10). Jesus himself alluded afterward to both incidents (8:14–21). Each time a tremendous sensation was the result, though the disciples failed to understand the lessons taught by these acted parables (8:19 ff.).

Mark tells of the fear of the disciples when they saw Jesus coming to them walking on the water (6:45–52): "For they all saw him, and were troubled." Even after Jesus was in the boat, "they were sore amazed in themselves." On the plain of Gennesaret the people crowded around Jesus to touch the hem of his garment (6:53–56).

One of the neatest turns in Mark's Gospel is the story of the Greek woman's wit in repartee and strong faith that won the blessing of Christ for her little Gentile daughter (7:24–30).

The picturesque style of Mark comes out well in the case of the blind man who was healed by degrees and at first saw men as trees walking and then, after a second touch from Christ, clearly. Jesus did not hesitate to touch him a second time (8:22–26).

The failure of the disciples to heal the epileptic boy almost destroyed the father's faith in Jesus (9:9–29). The disciples failed from lack of prayer, as we so often do now. We do not even have faith equal to a grain of mustard seed when we go up against "this mountain."

One can see and hear poor blind Bartimeus on the Jericho road as he cried out to Jesus of Nazareth who was passing by (10:46–52). In grateful joy he sprang up and followed Jesus with the rest on toward Jerusalem.

The cursing of the withered fig tree (11:12–14, 20–26) puzzled the disciples, for the tree was not responsible for its having leaves before figs. But this also is an acted parable, an object lesson for them and for us. We must not advertise what we do not have. "By their fruits ye shall know them." The wonder of Jesus is not explained. He is himself greater than all his miracles, Son of God and Son of man.

VI

The Christ of Mark's Gospel

Peter answereth and saith unto him, Thou art the Christ.   MARK 8:29.

1. *Mark Responsible for Our Picture of Christ.*—It is eminently worth our while to look at the picture of Christ in Mark's Gospel. If John's Gospel is the latest, Mark's is the earliest. It is generally held that Mark is later than Q and may have used Q, but we do not actually have Q except as a matter of critical analysis. However, we do possess Mark. Not all the critics yet agree that our canonical Mark was written by John Mark. The Ur-Marcus theory still has a following. Others favor the Redactor theory involving a considerable revision of the original Mark (by John Mark). The purpose of this chapter is not to go again into a discussion of Mark's Gospel and the Synoptic problem.

We may let the question rest for our purposes now with the conclusion that nothing can be urged against the unanimous tradition that the Second Gospel was written by John Mark. We must, however, concern ourselves for a moment with the view frequently expressed by the liberals that Mark is responsible for uniting the Palestinian tradition about the human hero and leader of a Jewish reform movement with the Hellenistic conception of the divine Christ of Pauline theology. It is assumed that Mark is chiefly responsible for giving permanent form to the theologizing about Jesus which made a divine Christ out of a human being.

59

We have passed through the "Jesus or Christ" controversy. But the alternative will not stand sober criticism. Jesus is the Christ of Mark, Matthew, Luke, John, Paul, Peter, James, Jude, and the author of Hebrews. We went through the "back to Christ" cry to get away from the Pauline Christ and the Johannine Christ. The Synoptic Christ was what was wanted. But, lo, he is the same in outline as the Johannine and the Pauline Christ. It is now clear that Paul did not "invent" Christ out of the Jesus of history. Criticism has discovered Q, the main source of discourses of Jesus in Matthew and Luke, used on a par with Mark's Gospel by them, possibly used even by Mark. But the picture of Jesus in Q is the same in fundamental outlines as that in the Synoptic Gospels.

2. *The Note of Reality.*—The liberal is unwilling to admit that Mark's picture of Christ is veracious. The distinction between Mark, the other two synoptists, and John is only relative. The Christ of the first three Gospels is seen as a real man and not yet as God become man. It is held that in comparison with the other Gospels, Mark simply represents an earlier stage of apologetic tendency and thus a comparatively clearer presentation of tradition.

Others hold that the Gospel of Mark is the most Pauline of the Synoptic Gospels and that the dominant idea of the author was to bring about belief in Jesus Christ as the Son of God. This may be admitted without in the least discrediting the historical worth of Mark's Gospel. There is small use for any man to write a book unless he has a serious purpose in view. It is true that all the Gospels have an apologetic value. The same thing is true of every scientific paper that supports a thesis.

But while this is true, Mark's Christ has the note of reality. It is true that Peter's preaching lies behind the Second Gospel, though the book is not a mere translation of Peter's

Aramaic discourses. Mark has made a real book but without destroying the freshness of Peter's picture of Jesus. Peter made Mark see Jesus with great vividness and power, and he has preserved the startling boldness of that image. Mark himself was not a theologian with a touch of philosophy like John or a scholarly historian like Luke or a man of affairs with his tabulated lists like Matthew. He took his task to be rather that of the reporter of the great apostle, Simon Peter, the glowing preacher whose warmth and color greatly moved Mark's heart and life as well as thousands of other lives.

The reports of Peter's discourses in Acts 2 and 10 make it easy to believe that Peter's hearers in Rome and elsewhere besought Mark to write out his recollections of these wonderful addresses. If we wish to get a clear idea of the way that the early disciples portrayed Jesus in their sermons, we may obtain that conception in Mark's Gospel. It is the preacher's picture of Christ, the preacher who knew Jesus by blessed experience and who was trying to win others to the service of Christ. Paul reminded the Galatians, "before whose eyes Jesus Christ was openly set forth crucified" (Gal. 3:1), of his own picturesque preaching of Christ.

3. *Mark's Purpose in this Gospel.*—We have in Mark's Gospel our earliest picture of Christ in any adequate sense, for Q is only a torso. It is of supreme importance for us all to look at Mark's Christ with clear eyes and open hearts and honest minds. It is held by some that the opening words of this Gospel (1:1) constitute a mere headline and were not a part of the original Mark. But whether the present headline of the Gospel is due to Mark or to an early editor, it admirably expresses the idea of the book. *It is the Gospel of Jesus Christ, the Son of God.* It is thus not exactly "The Life of Christ According to Mark."

Mark does not undertake to give us the life of Christ but

the message of Jesus in its essential features and enough of his claims and acts to prove that Jesus is in reality "the Christ, the Son of God," though not all the manuscripts have the phrase "the Son of God." We must not be misled into thinking that Mark has given us, or meant to give us, a collection of the words of Jesus. What he has done for us is to present Christ in action both as worker and as teacher. We see Jesus as the man of power, and it is the power of God and not of a mere man. Mark has little theology in his book in the sense of theological or philosophical terms, and yet all the fundamental doctrines concerning the person and work of Christ are here. He does not conceal his own opinion about Jesus, though there is no abstract discussion as one finds in a modern treatise. It will not do to depreciate Mark's method as wholly lacking in merit because he is more objective and concrete. The peculiar vitality of this Gospel is partly due to this very fact. Mark's picture of Christ stirs the mind to intense activity and is creative of the truest theology.

4. *Limitations in Mark's Gospel.*—The limitations of Mark's Gospel confront us at once. There is nothing about the birth and infancy of Jesus. What conclusion shall we draw from this fact? The argument from silence is notoriously precarious. The only just conclusion is that Mark used the material at hand that suited his purpose. He omits also the first year of the public ministry after the baptism and temptation, if we accept, as I do, John's Gospel as reliable history. We may suppose that Mark followed the general plan of Peter's discourses with chief emphasis on the Galilean ministry and Passion Week which Peter employed in Caesarea (Acts 10:34–43). It is quite gratuitous to say that the narratives in Matthew and Luke are religious legends of no historical value because Mark is silent. Such a view simply indicates that its proponent has made up his

mind about the situation without regard to the available facts.

Mark simply has nothing to say on that subject and cannot be properly quoted as hostile to that view of Christ's birth.

5. *The Messianic Consciousness.*—Mark presents Jesus as the Baptist's successor. He is the herald of the kingdom, taking up the work of John. This is true, but Mark does not make John the chief figure and Jesus the secondary follower. The attitude of John toward Jesus is distinctly that of the forerunner whose whole mission was absorbed in the work of the Messiah. "There cometh after me he that is mightier than I, the latchet of whose shoes I am not worthy to stoop down and unloose" (Mark 1:7). John stood alone, but he pointed to the really great One whose very baptism would surpass his own (1:8). It will not do, therefore, to say that in Mark the messiahship of Jesus is a development and not claimed at the start as in John's Gospel.

There is more truth in the idea that in Jerusalem the issue was joined at once between Christ and the Pharisees while in Galilee Jesus held the matter in abeyance as long as possible. But this is not to say that Jesus himself was at first unaware of the real nature of his person and mission or that the disciples did not at once take him as Messiah, as John's Gospel represents them as doing. The disciples did not grasp the spiritual character of the Messianic kingdom, not until Pentecost came with the Spirit's illumination, for even after the resurrection of Jesus they still clung to the pharisaic conception of a political kingdom (Acts 1:6).

Jesus did test the disciples concerning their knowledge of his person toward the close of the summer of withdrawal from Galilee (Mark 8:27 ff.), but it is probable that he wished to know now whether they still believed in him as the Messiah after all that they had seen and heard. Even then he charged them not to tell what Peter had so nobly said. Least of all is it proper to say that Mark's Gospel treats Jesus simply as a man who was carried away by the enthusiasm of the multitude and by his own excitement to make abnormal claims for himself at the close of his career. That is not the way the Second Gospel portrays Jesus. There is a tendency among some scholars to interpret the historical notices in the Gospel of Mark as if they give no indication of the declaration of Jesus· about his ministry. It is assumed that he had no consciousness at all of a definite mission and simply took events as they came, making the most of them. I do not so read Mark's Gospel.

Let us see. In the "headline" (1:1) Jesus is termed the "Christ, the Son of God." John the Baptist foretold the coming One as near and as the expected great One, though Mark does not say that he applied to him the word "Messiah" (1:2–8). But we must not be slaves of a word. The idea of the Messiah is in the context. At the baptism of Jesus (1:9–11) by the Baptist the Spirit descended on him as a dove and the Father addressed Jesus as "my beloved Son," and this act of baptism called forth the approval of the Father. The Baptist heard God's voice salute Jesus as the Son of God. This language must mean the Messiah and presents the highest conception of that office. The doctrine of the Trinity is really here (Father, Son, Spirit). It will not do to say that Jesus was not yet conscious of his mission and of his peculiar relation to God. Thus at the very beginning of our earliest Gospel all the essential elements in the person and work of Christ confront us. His humanity is here and his deity is here. The messianic consciousness of Jesus is inevitably involved. This great event made the Baptist certain that he had made no mistake in his identification of Jesus as the Messiah. There were no disciples of Jesus as yet.

Mark does not give the story of the temptation of Jesus by Satan where the deity of Jesus is subtly challenged by the devil and where his humanity is strongly emphasized by the weakness of hunger. But the fact of the temptation is given by Mark with a touch of loneliness added by the mention of "the wild beasts" as his companions and the comfort of the angels at the end (1:12 f.). Certainly in Matthew and Luke, Jesus stands pitted against the prince of this world who at once perceives that he is dealing with the Son of God, and Jesus is fully conscious of his own personality and of the vast issues at stake in the conflict. There is nothing in the Gospel of John that more thoroughly pictures the deity of Christ than the temptation where his humanity is so powerfully attacked by Satan.

When the demons hailed Jesus as "the Holy One of God" (1:24), Jesus made no disclaimer but commanded silence, for such testimony would not help his cause. The restraint of Jesus in Galilee does not, therefore, mean doubt on his own part about his messiahship or ignorance on the part of the early disciples but only that for prudential reasons Jesus did not make such formal and public claims. The public in Galilee were too fanatical to permit it without precipitating a crisis. The intensity of the popular excitement is manifest in the early Galilean ministry. "They were all amazed" (1:27); "all the city was gathered together at the door" (1:33); "all are seeking thee" (1:37); "Jesus could no more openly enter into a city, but was without in desert places: and they came to him from every quarter" (1:45). It is evident that everywhere people were hailing Jesus as the Messiah proclaimed by the Baptist, though Jesus avoided the use of the term.

6. *Son of God and Son of Man.*—The Pharisees from Jerusalem were quick to see the inevitable implication of the claims and works of Jesus. When Jesus said to the par-

alytic let down through the tile roof, "Son, thy sins are forgiven" (Mark 2:5), they were instant with the accusation in their hearts, "He blasphemeth: who can forgive sins but one, even God?" (2:7). In this tense atmosphere Jesus proceeded to heal the man to prove his power and authority to forgive sins and so his equality with God. "But that ye may know that the Son of man hath authority on earth to forgive sins (he saith to the sick of the palsy), I say unto thee, Arise, take up thy bed, and go into thy house" (2:10 f.). There is no possibility of misunderstanding the import of this language. The use of the phrase "the Son of man" instead of "Messiah" probably kept the populace from clearly understanding the messianic claim that Jesus made and robbed the Pharisees of a technical charge of blasphemy. But some of them probably knew that the phrase already had a messianic sense in their apocalyptic writings, and all of them knew that Jesus really claimed practical equality with God and, worst of all, defied them and proved his power by healing the paralytic to the amazement of the crowd who "glorified God, saying, We never saw it on this fashion" (2:12).

In the first two chapters, therefore, we meet the use of "Son of God" and "Son of man," which aptly describe the deity and the humanity of Jesus. Tremendous efforts have been made to empty them of any real meaning. But in Mark's Gospel "the Son of God" means more than just any man, since all men are sons of God in one sense. "Son of man" can be a translation of the Aramaic *barnasha,* a man, any man, but that idea is puerile and jejune in most of the passages from the mouth of Jesus. Christ is not in 2:10 showing that any man has the power to forgive sins but that *he* has that authority. We have in Mark no definition of the phrase "the Son of man," but it is manifestly messianic and representative. The reality of Christ's humanity

66

is clearly stated by it, but a great deal more. He is, besides, the representative man of the race and the ideal man. By means of this term, of which Jesus was fond, he is able to lay claim to the messiahship without using the word "Messiah," which would give instant offense to the rulers and which would at once arouse the passion of the people. How much the twelve apostles understood at first by the language of Jesus we are not told. But we must remember that they also heard him called "the Son of God" and, as John's Gospel shows, had special teaching from Jesus concerning his messiahship.

Jesus early foresaw and foretold his death, according to Mark's Gospel, for he spoke of the fasting after the death of the bridegroom (2:20). His claim to lordship of the sabbath (2:27 f.) probably astonished the disciples as much as it angered Christ's enemies. The unclean spirits had the habit of making the demoniacs fall down before Jesus, crying, "Thou art the Son of God" (3:11). Some impression was probably made on the minds of some by this testimony.

7. *Adverse Opinions.*—Mark does not hesitate to present the adverse opinions about Jesus. "His friends . . . went out to lay hold on him: for they said, He is beside himself" (3:21). This was the charitable construction placed on Christ's conduct by his own "brothers" (3:31) when they heard the bitter accusation of the Pharisees from Jerusalem that Jesus was in league with the devil (3:22). Apparently for the moment even Mary, the mother of Jesus, felt that the strain had been too great upon Jesus. She came with her sons, "calling him," to take him home. This dark scene is characteristic of Mark's method. He puts in the light and shadow of the actual life of Jesus, not because he is in doubt, but simply as an artist true to the life.

Over against this depreciation of Jesus Mark put the exceeding fear of the disciples in the boat, "Who then is this, that even the wind and the sea obey him?" (4:41). They had doubtless long before this taken Jesus as the Messiah, but they had no well-defined Christology apart from the pharisaic environment. They were in confusion over the apparent contradiction between the sleeping and drowning Jesus and the Master of wind and wave. Soon the disciples saw the wild man of the tombs run and fall down and worship Jesus as he screamed, "What have I to do with thee, Jesus, thou Son of the Most High God?" (5:7). Huxley's ridicule of the "Gadarene pig affair" in his debate with Gladstone has not disposed of the weird power of this scene. Peter seems to have been greatly moved by it, for Mark's narrative is wonderfully vivid and dramatic.

The contrasts in Christ's person in Mark's Gospel appear with great clearness between the sensitiveness of Christ to the loss of energy as power went out from him at the touch of his garment by the sick woman (5:30 f.) and the tender mastery over death in the house of Jairus where in the presence of a small group Jesus restored the child to life. Mark has kept the very Aramaic words that Jesus used to the little girl, *Talitha cumi* (5:41). Peter never forgot them, as for the first time he saw Jesus as the conqueror of death.

The picture of Jesus in the synagogue in Nazareth (6:1–6) reveals the limitations in the work of the Master. His old friends and neighbors looked upon Jesus as a wonder since he sprang from the midst of them. He was to them still "the carpenter" and not the Messiah. They felt that there must be some mistake about his gifts and graces since they had discovered none of them while he was with them. Many another man has been a stumblingblock to his neighbors, for "a prophet is not without honor, save in his own country" (6:4). The lack of faith limited the power of Jesus to work miracles.

People differed in their interpretation of Jesus then as

68

now, but all had to form some opinion about him. The third Galilean campaign attracted the attention of Herod Antipas, whose guilty fears made him think that Jesus was John the Baptist come to life again. Others thought that Jesus was Elijah or another of the prophets. Some felt that he was indeed the Messiah, as the Baptist had said. Mark shows his fidelity as a historian in letting us see that Jesus did not convince all that he was the Son of God, the Son of man. He seemed to most only a wonderful man. There was no doubt of his humanity. His deity was evident enough for those who had eyes to see and ears to hear, but his deity was to be held in harmony with his humanity, however little we may be able to explain the union. Mark does not undertake to explain; he states the facts as he got hold of them and lets the facts speak for themselves.

8. *The Disciples Puzzled.*—The disciples themselves were repeatedly puzzled by the conduct of Jesus. Mark shows this with sheer simplicity and *naïveté*. Jesus was weary with the apostles and sought rest but rallied and taught the eager crowds. He revealed himself as Lord of nature as he multiplied the loaves and the fishes for the multitude (6:30–44) and then walked upon the water to the frightened disciples (6:45–52). Even more, "they were sore amazed in themselves" as they tried to understand Jesus and his works. It was not a simple matter to comprehend Jesus Christ, though these men saw him day by day. Their eyes "were holden," we read, holden by their preconceived ideas about the Messiah and by their own theological interpretations of Jesus.

The patience of Jesus was sorely tried by the slow progress of the disciples in grasping the real significance of his teaching about himself. They stumbled in simple matters like the use of leaven for teaching (8:15), but they did hold on to the great truth that Jesus claimed to be the

69

Messiah (8:27–30), however imperfect their views of the Messiah were. This at least was something to be grateful for, and Jesus charged the apostles not to tell others as yet what they knew. The masses were fickle and volatile and would only take Jesus as a political Messiah in accord with pharisaic theology.

Mark does not enlarge upon Peter's great confession as Matthew does, but shows that Peter was the spokesman on this important occasion. Perhaps Peter had not discoursed upon the words of Jesus to him at this eventful juncture. But Peter, as Mark has it (8:31–33), did tell of Christ's calling him "Satan" for his presumptuous advice. The mystery of Jesus appeared to grow as he discussed his own death after the staunch avowal of faith in his messiahship and divine sonship. In his rebuke of Peter, Jesus proceeded to set forth the true philosophy of life and death. This was applicable to the Son of man most of all as he faced his own cross, and yet this Son of man was to come "in the glory of his Father with the holy angels" (8:38). He will come to judge those who are ashamed of him here and to bless those who confess him. This was no ordinary "son of man" (*barnasha*) who was himself the test of every man's life and destiny, Saviour and Judge of all. It is by his Father's glory that he is the Son of God, and yet he will judge mankind as the Son of man whose ideal he is. Mark is fully conscious that he is not presenting the portraiture of a mere Jewish prophet or Galilean teacher. He is the greatest of all teachers, the supreme prophet of the ages, the model for human life, the brother of the race. But he is far more than all this. Mark makes it evident that this "more" is what makes all the rest possible and offers hope to men.

9. *Christ's Conception of His Death.*—The scene on the Mount of Transfiguration (9:2–13) reveals Jesus in his glory

as he talks with Moses and Elijah, representatives of law and prophecy, not on a par with them but as their superior. He is addressed by the Father's voice as "my beloved Son," while he alludes to himself in his talk with the three disciples as "the Son of man." Mark represents the death of Christ as the theme of the high converse with Moses and Elijah. Jesus had failed to make the disciples comprehend the import of his atoning death as they continued to fail in this supreme matter.

To the disciples it was incongruous and incomprehensible that the Messiah should die. They had as yet no room for the suffering Messiah in their theology. They could see how he was prophet and king but not how he was priest. And yet the priestly aspect of Christ's work is the chief thing as he conceived it. His sacrificial death was the real purpose of his earthly life. He came to give life to men, but this gift of life was made possible by his own death. With this spirit Christ approached his own death. He had to drink this cup and to receive the baptism of death (10:38). "For the Son of man also came not to be ministered unto, but to minister, and to give his life a ransom for many" (10:45). Jesus did not often allude to this deepest aspect of his work, for the disciples could not become reconciled to the fact of his death. They were poorly prepared as yet for the interpretation of that death. But it is significant that in Mark's Gospel the atonement finds a real place. Evidently it had this place in Peter's preaching (cf. Acts 2:38; 10:43) as in his epistles (1 Pet. 1:18 f.). As Jesus went on to Jerusalem to meet his hour, he saw that his death was to be a "ransom for many." The papyri have this word (*lutron*) as the price paid for freeing a slave. So Jesus looked upon his death. When he instituted the supper after the last passover meal, he said, "This is my blood of the covenant, which is poured out for many" (14:24).

71

This view is no afterthought with Jesus, no last resort of a disappointed man who sought refuge in death after defeat in life. It is not the later theologizing of Peter or of Mark. It is Peter's recollection of the words of Jesus, which Peter frankly confessed that he did not at the time understand. Nothing is more true to life in Mark's Gospel than his retention of the confession and dullness of the apostles concerning the teaching of Jesus about his personal work. The development in this Gospel, as in John's Gospel, is chiefly in the revelation of Jesus to these awakening men in the face of the growing hostility of his enemies. The atmospheric environment was all against the true perception of the nature of the Messiah whom they loved and adored. The mystery deepened as they entered further with Christ into the shadow of the cross. Their hearts beat back and forth as they shared the shifting scenes of the closing days. The triumphal entry was a public proclamation of the messiahship of Jesus. The Jerusalem authorities so interpreted it. And Jesus meant them to so understand it. The people hailed Jesus with utter joy as "he that cometh in the name of the Lord" (11:9). And yet Jesus knew that he was not the political Messiah that they took him to be, knew also that to let it pass that way would give his enemies the charge against him that they wished. From the standpoint of the Sanhedrin, he was a blasphemer for claiming to be the Messiah.

From the standpoint of Rome, he could be charged with high treason in setting himself up as a rival king to Caesar. Jesus foresaw all this and yet made his defiance on purpose. Thus he would force the hand of his enemies and bring matters to a crisis and reveal their guilt, and so he would meet his hour as the Lamb of God offered on the cross for human sin. The sinlessness of Christ is taught in Mark, as well as the voluntariness of his death. The dignity of the great tragedy is here. Jesus is master of the Temple and orders the money-changers out (11:15). In the parable of the husbandman and the vineyard Jesus shows that he is the King's Son, to the dismay of his enemies. He applies to himself the words of the psalmist (118:22 f.) that the stone which the builders rejected is become the head of the corner (Mark 12:10). He shows that David's son is also David's Lord, with clear implication concerning his own humanity and deity as the Messiah (12:35–37), to the anger of the rulers and the joy of the common people.

10. *Victor on the Cross.*—In the eschatological discourse, the so-called "little apocalypse," in the very verse wherein he admits his ignorance of the time of his second coming and of the world's judgment he affirms his peculiar sonship (13:32), as in John's Gospel. Almost in the hour of his death he asserts his lordship and victory over all his foes in the end: "And then shall they see the Son of man coming in clouds with great power and glory" (13:26).

He never seemed more completely master of his own destiny than when he was the victim of human hate. He is Lord of the world that crucifies him. He is adjudged guilty of blasphemy and of treason, though free from all sin, and will some day come as Judge of his judges and of all men. Jesus was conscious that he was laying down his life for the world's sin, but he by no means held those guiltless who compassed his death. "For the Son of man goeth, even as it is written of him: but woe unto that man through whom the Son of man is betrayed! good were it for that man if he had not been born" (14:21). "The hour is come; behold, the Son of man is betrayed into the hands of sinners" (14:41).

In the hour of weakness in the garden of Gethsemane when the soul of Jesus shrank from the cup of woe, he yet was fully conscious that he was God's Son and began his

73

heart-rending plea and absolute submission to the Father's will with the tender words, "Abba, Father" (14:36), blending the Aramaic of his childhood and the Greek, as did Paul in Romans 8:15 and Galatians 4:6.

In the trial before Caiaphas and the Sanhedrin Jesus on oath confessed that he is "the Christ, the Son of the Blessed" (14:61), when he knew that this confession meant his death. But Jesus would not renounce his true personality to save his mortal life. In this very moment Jesus claimed also to be the Son of man whom Caiaphas and his other judges will one day see "sitting at the right hand of Power," as King by the side of the Father on the throne, "and coming with the clouds of heaven" (14:62). This defiance of Caiaphas was ample proof to him of blasphemy. But it shows beyond controversy that Mark gives us the high conception of the person of Christ.

The claims of Jesus were flung in his teeth as he hung on the cross. His enemies defied "the Christ, the King of Israel" to come down from the cross (15:32). In mockery they unconsciously stated the great truth about his whole work: "He saved others; himself he cannot save" (15:31).

In the cry of agony, "My God, my God, why hast thou forsaken me?" we seem to see the surprise of Jesus that his Father should allow him to walk this path alone, even to pay the debt of the sin of the race and to make redemption possible. But his very death impressed a Roman centurion that he was surely God's Son (15:39). The death of Jesus was no swoon but actual death, and the disciples were all in despair in this hour of gloom.

The closing verses of our Mark (16:9–20) are not found in the oldest documents. We cannot, therefore, appeal to them with confidence in proof of the resurrection of Jesus. But in Mark 16:1–8 the fact of the resurrection is made plain. The women found the tomb empty, but a young man in a white robe proclaimed that Jesus is risen from the dead and has sent a special message to "his disciples and Peter" (16:7). The Gospel closes with Peter reinstated in Christ's confidence and with Jesus as the risen Lord who will carry on and carry out his great program for the world's redemption.

It is true that in Mark's Gospel we possess a mere sketch of the life and work, person and principles of Jesus. And yet it is also true that in this sketch we have the main features of the Christ of Matthew, Luke, and John. "These and similar sayings contain an almost complete outline of Christian soteriology and eschatology, and assert the principles of the new life which the Lord taught and exemplified and which His Spirit was to produce in the life of the future Church."

The marvel of it all is the fact that it is done in such short compass, with such clarity, with such vividness (almost vivacity), and with such power. The stamp of reality is in this story. To be sure, the supernatural is here, and Jesus is offered to us as a supernatural person without apology. But the day is gone when the Gospels can be refused a hearing because of the presence of the supernatural in them. If God exists, it is unhistorical and unscientific to ignore him. The Christ of Mark is the Christ of the believer in all the ages. He asks that his power over life be put to the test of experience before one decides that he is not the Son of God.

There is pathos in the fact that the friends of Jesus did not see at first the true import of his claims. His enemies saw the peril to their theology and power in the revolutionary reforms with his messianic assumptions. Mark has presented the graphic story with dramatic power, but there is no mistaking his meaning. He proves the deity of Jesus in his own way as conclusively as the Gospel of John does.

VII

Jesus in Mark's Gospel the Exemplar for Preachers

Come ye after me, and I will make you to become fishers of men. MARK 1:17.

Modern preachers are greatly interested in the first portrayal of the greatest preacher of all time, Jesus of Nazareth. He is the model for all preachers. He is, to be sure, much more than this. He is Son of God, Son of man, Lord and Saviour, and he is all of this in Mark's Gospel. But he was a preacher, and his message and work as a preacher are presented with great clearness and power in this Gospel of action. Mark has no formal discussion of this aspect of Christ's work, but we see him in action as a preacher. We see the whole task of the modern preacher reflected in this picture of Christ drawn by Mark. It is not the homiletics of Jesus that we are primarily concerned with in this chapter, though that is interesting and we catch glimpses of it now and then. Jesus is so many-sided in his human nature that it is good to look at him sometimes from this one angle of vision. Let us see, then, how Mark describes Jesus the preacher.

1. *Pictured by a Preacher.*—Mark's portraiture of Christ comes mainly from the reminiscences of Simon Peter, as nearly all modern scholars agree. The testimony of Papias

and various other early writers is explicit on this point, as we have seen. There are many proofs of the work of an eyewitness in the Gospel of Mark. Peter was most of all a preacher. He lacked the intellectual strength and grasp of Paul, but he was a man of quick insight, a practical turn, a warm heart, and sympathy. Mark was Peter's disciple and interpreter and heard Peter preach Jesus with all his fervor and freshness. The fidelity of Mark is shown by the wonderful skill with which he has preserved the many nuances in Peter's glowing oratory. The Christ of Mark is Christ as Peter knows him by blessed fellowship and under the tutelage of the Holy Spirit. Peter did not hide his own weaknesses and shortcomings in his preaching, and Mark has kept them in his story. They give life and color to the narrative.

2. *Mightier than the Baptist.*—The very first thing in Mark's Gospel is his bold sketch of John the Baptist, "who baptized in the wilderness and preached the baptism of repentance unto remission of sins" (1:4). This picturesque preacher of righteousness summoned the Jewish nation to repentance and treated them as Gentiles by demanding that they submit to baptism, confessing their sins. It was sensational enough to draw all Jerusalem and all Judea to the wilderness by the Jordan. He preached as a herald and kept it up (imperfect tense) with the startling announcement, "There cometh after me he that is mightier than I, the latchet of whose shoes I am not worthy to stoop down and unloose" (1:7). John said this at the very acme of his popularity, when all men held him to be a prophet (11:32) and some wondered if he were not himself the Messiah.

John was a mighty preacher, as the ages testify. The few pages in the Gospels that give John's message justify the praise of Jesus and the enthusiasm of the multitudes. John is one of the outstanding preachers of all history. But he

77

felt that his chief glory was to be the forerunner of the great Preacher. John's word is "stronger." It was not an anemic Messiah that he foresaw but a man of transcendent energy and power, who "shall baptize you in the Holy Spirit" (1:8). Did Christ fulfil John's forecast? The first time that he saw him he beheld the Holy Spirit come upon him like a dove and heard the voice from heaven greet him as God's beloved Son (1:10 f.). That was an introduction in keeping with John's vision.

3. *Tempted Like Other Preachers.*—Preachers know that they are not exempt from temptation. Some may imagine that they are immune from the darts of the devil, but they are soon undeceived. Judas at last fell a victim to the wiles of the devil, and Peter was in dire peril. for Jesus said to him, "Satan asked to have you, that he might sift you as wheat: but I made supplication for thee, that thy faith fail not" (Luke 22:31 f.). The complacency of Peter was shared by all the twelve, but the result with Peter was very sad. In the agony in Gethsemane Jesus recurred to his anxiety: "Pray that ye enter not into temptation" (Luke 22:40). Jesus was feeling again the devil's power as at the beginning of his ministry when the Spirit drove him into the wilderness when he was tempted by Satan. Mark's language is almost daring. He does not say that the Spirit drove Jesus into temptation (1:12), but it is a bold statement of the submission of Jesus to the leading of the Holy Spirit. Matthew does say, "Then was Jesus led up of the Spirit into the wilderness to be tempted of the devil" (4:1).

Certainly Jesus was conscious of what was ahead of him and apparently had a natural reluctance to meet the great adversary in mortal combat. Mark adds that Jesus "was with the wild beasts" (1:13), a weird picture of the lonely struggle with the tempter. "Angels came and ministered unto him" after the devil was vanquished, Matthew explains (4:11). The point for all preachers here is this: The devil did not spare Jesus himself. He will not hesitate to try his power upon each of us. It actually seems that the devil is particularly fond of compassing the downfall of a preacher. Paul warns Timothy and other preachers against "the snare of the devil" (1 Tim. 3:7). He sets traps for preachers. Jesus knew what it was to meet the devil at the very start and all through his ministry to the final victory (Luke 4:13).

4. *Preaching the Gospel of God.*—This language is Mark's first comment about Jesus when he "came into Galilee, preaching the gospel [good news] of God." (1:14). He had already pictured the Baptist "preaching the baptism of repentance unto remission of sins" (1:4). The new preacher took up the message of the forerunner, these two heralds of the dawn being thus linked in a noble succession: "The time is fulfilled, and the kingdom of God is at hand: repent ye, and believe in the gospel" (1:15). The Baptist was already in prison, but Jesus, undismayed, cried aloud with the same message in Galilee.

Preachers through all the ages have been thrown into prison and put to death, but that has not stopped other preachers from preaching. The moral courage of the preacher places him above kings and Caesars if he has the message of God. John had it, Jesus had it, Paul had it. Each in turn forfeited his life for the truth that he preached, but that truth has transformed the world. Newspapers and books have not destroyed the power of the preacher of the gospel of God. "Believe in the gospel," Jesus said. It does matter what one believes and what he preaches. The message of Jesus shook Galilee and is shaking the world today.

5. *Fishing for Fishers of Men.*—The very first incident that Mark records in the Galilean ministry is the call of Simon and Andrew, James and John (1:16–20). They were fishers, and Zebedee, father of James and John, employed

hired servants and seems to have been at the head of a fish company. It was not the first time that this group had seen Jesus, as we know from John's Gospel (1:34–42), but until now they had not definitely given up their calling as fishermen. "Come ye after me, and I will make you to become fishers of men." These four laymen (businessmen) gave up their business, profitable in all probability, to follow Jesus and help him win men.

The art of catching men for Christ is the supreme test of the evangelistic preacher. It has to be learned. Jesus undertook to teach these fishers how to fish for men. No calling is comparable in dignity with this. Jesus kept his promise. We know something of Peter's work on the great Pentecostal day and afterwards. John fished in a different way and wrote the wondrous spiritual Gospel that is still winning men to Christ. James became the first martyr among the twelve. We know less of Andrew, but he was a man of counsel. Each had his own way of fishing for men. It is a part of every preacher's work to find other fishers. Paul saw the same necessity and urges it upon Timothy in his last epistle. "The same commit thou to faithful men, who shall be able to teach others also" (2 Tim. 2:2). Jesus saw the need of it at the very beginning of his work in Galilee. It is the insistent call now upon modern men. The fields were never so white for the harvest, but the laborers are lamentably few. We must go fishing for fishers of men.

6. *Teaching with the Note of Authority.*—The first echo in Mark (1:22–28) of the teaching of Jesus in Galilee is the astonishment of the crowds in the synagogue. "They were astonished at his teaching: for he taught them as having authority, and not as the scribes" (1:22). Jesus was both teacher and preacher. Every preacher ought to be a teacher. These two aspects of one's work are not quite the same, but both ought to be present in varying proportions. Jesus is

called teacher in the Gospels more frequently than preacher. He came to be known as the Teacher (the Master). Both head and heart entered into his work. Mere instruction without warmth and passion will not win a hearing. Mere passion without teaching will not stick, and the passion will be torn to tatters. Both light and heat are demanded in the modern teacher-preacher. Jesus passed as a rabbi, though not a technical schoolman.

He was an irregular rabbi, but his message and method stood out in sharp contrast with the way the pharisaic rabbis or scribes taught in the synagogues. Jesus was allowed the courtesy of addressing the audiences in the synagogues. We know from the Talmud what the rabbinical method of instruction was. Both in the *Halachah* (the legal rules) and in the *Haggadah* (the explanatory and anecdotal comments) the scribe was very slow to take a position that he could not support by quotations from other rabbis. His discourse was largely a string of quotations and lacked independence and the personal quality that gives charm and magnetism. Jesus was like a breeze from the hills in his originality, outlook, and freshness of statement. "What is this? a new teaching! with authority he commandeth even the unclean spirits, and they obey him" (1:27).

There is little room today for the mere dogmatist, but there is still less in modern preaching for the spineless doubter who has no convictions and no power with God or men or over demons. Jesus stood in the synagogue, the master over the forces of evil and the master of men's consciences which he challenged to new service for God and man. Without the note of authority the preacher is a helpless jellyfish. It cannot be feigned. It comes only with the possession of truth and is the note of reality.

7. *A Healing Ministry.*—The preaching of Jesus had a charm all its own, the spell of which is still upon the world.

But it is probable that his healing ministry created more enthusiasm and excitement than his teaching, wondrous as that was. Physicians there were, but they were woefully primitive in many of their methods and in much of their knowledge. Medical knowledge has made great strides in recent years, but people are still living who can recall the leeches and bleeding processes of a preceding generation of physicians. Theology for long was literally queen of the sciences, for physical science was slow in progressing. Theology is still queen of the sciences in importance and rejoices in the great progress made in the treatment of the ills of body and mind.

Jesus is still the Great Physician of the ages, equally at home in the treatment of the sin-sick soul and the pain-racked body. People flocked to him with their ills as they do to our medical missionaries today. Some had chronic troubles like the poor woman who "had suffered many things of many physicians, and had spent all that she had, and was nothing bettered, but rather grew worse" (Mark 5:26). She closely resembles people today who go from one quack to another, for they existed then as now. Once more her hope revived, as she heard of the cures (real cures this time) of the new healer. So she slipped up behind Jesus and touched his garment with simple faith. "If I touch but his garments, I shall be made whole" (5:28). Jesus felt power go from him as she was healed. It cost Christ something to heal the sick as well as to save the lost.

Christianity has two sides to its work, the ministry to the soul and the ministry to the body. Jesus combined them, and we must do the same. It does not follow that the modern preacher should be a physician or should be a professional faith-healer. Paul the preacher and Luke the physician worked together. So the Christian preacher and the Christian physician should co-operate in their work for the whole man. Hospitals are a fit expression of the spirit of Jesus. Jesus did not make the cure of the body his chief task, but he showed mercy upon the suffering at every turn, and it is an empty Christianity today that does not enter into the Red Cross spirit. The cross of Jesus has a message for the soul and the body.

8. *Hindered by His Popularity.*—Early in the Galilean ministry the great crowds pressed upon Jesus in such throngs that he felt them as a hindrance to his work. So he sought relief in prayer, rising long before day and going out to a desert place to pray, only to have Peter rush upon him with the cry, "All are seeking thee" (1:35 ff.). Time and again the pressure of the crowds caused Jesus to seek the woods and the fields and communion with the Father. "Jesus could no more openly enter into a city, but was without in desert places: and they came to him from every quarter" (1:45).

The peril of the crowd is felt by every popular preacher. To be sure, there is danger in the absence of the people, danger of a drying up of life and a slowing down of energy unless one keeps himself alive to the real greatness of his task in a small place so that he shall do a big work in a little place, which is far better than a little work in a big place. But many a preacher who has caught the ear of the crowd has lost the true perspective and has lived with the crowd too much. He has not followed the example of Jesus in going to the desert places, the secret places with God and nature, for spiritual renewal. Nature is good for the recuperation of the preacher's energy and for wholesome outlook upon the realities of life. It is poor economy for the busy preacher to neglect his books, his closet, his recreation. The crowds may upset his nerves, sap his energy, and rob him of his power. Then the crowds will leave him alone and for good.

9. *Seeking Rest and Finding Work.*—This has been the fate of many a tired preacher who hied him to the hills and found rest in work instead of repose. And yet absolute rest is sometimes required. Jesus sought it, and he made the twelve try it when they came back from the strenuous campaign through Galilee. "Come ye yourselves apart into a desert place, and rest a while. For there were many coming and going, and they had no leisure so much as to eat" (6:31). So they went off in the heat with Jesus to a desert place near Bethsaida-Julias where the grass was green on the mountainside, a lovely place for an outing with the Teacher. But the rest was rudely broken by the rush of the crowds round the lake. What was Jesus to do? He did not disappoint the multitudes, hungry for the bread of life. He had compassion on the people and, tired as he was, roused himself for the work of teaching and healing. Then they had a picnic on a grand scale as Jesus made the twelve act as waiters for the five thousand men besides women and children. Never mind now about this miracle of emergency.

Jesus was equal to every occasion, and the outcome stirred the people to the highest pitch of excitement. They wanted to make him king now without delay and to set up a kingdom independent of Rome. To escape from this predicament the Master sent the disciples home in the boat "while he himself sendeth the multitude away" (6:45). Then "he departed into the mountain to pray," to spend most of the night alone with the Father in the hills. That was refreshment for his spirit and for his body.

10. *Finding Difficulty in Teaching His Students.*—It is pathetic to see how hard it was for the twelve apostles, who were so close to the Master and so constantly with him, to learn the truth about his person and his message. They were at first the product of the pharisaic environment

of Palestine. All but Judas were from Galilee, which was less in the grip of the rabbis than Judea. But they all, even the spiritual John, found it difficult to brush aside the rabbinical cobwebs so cunningly spun around their heads. Jesus was patient with them and tried many expedients as a teacher. He taught them in public and in private.

He was himself the master teacher of all time and revealed all the pedagogical skill that other teachers gain more or less by long and laborious study. It was all spontaneous with Jesus. A greater than Aristotle was there, but these chosen men, the flower of the early days of the kingdom of God on earth, opened slowly to the rays of the sun. Sometimes they asked Jesus what he meant. "And when he was entered into the house from the multitude, his disciples asked of him the parable. And he saith unto them, Are ye so without understanding also?" (7:17 f.). Jesus took them with him out of Galilee for some months of special training, and still they failed to understand Christ's method. "Do ye not yet perceive, neither understand? have ye your heart hardened? Having eyes, see ye not? and having ears, hear ye not? and do ye not remember?" (8:17 f.). Every teacher can sympathize with Jesus at this point. And yet these men did finally come to know Jesus.

11. *Misunderstood by Some of His Friends.*—It is a hard lot for a preacher to be unappreciated at home by those who ought to love him most and to know him best. Jesus had the love and sympathy of his mother from the first and at the last, for she stood by the cross as he died with the sword through her heart, as Simeon had said would come to pass. But there was a time in the ministry of Jesus when many seemed to feel that the strain had become too great for her wondrous son.

The rabbis were saying that Jesus was in league with Beelzebub in explanation of his undoubted miracles. This she knew to be utterly untrue, but it was humiliating to her pride to hear him so maligned. He did act strangely at times. Sometimes the multitude pressed upon him so that he and they "could not so much as eat bread. And when his friends heard it, they went to lay hold on him: for they said, He is beside himself" (3:20 f.). This was the charitable construction of his conduct in opposition to the biting cynicism of the scribes (3:22). Finally "there come his mother and his brethren; and, standing without, they sent unto him, calling him" (3:31). Evidently they wished to take him home until he was calmer and came to himself.

It is not hard to imagine the agony in Mary's heart at this situation. The brothers probably felt a superiority to Jesus and a dislike for the unpleasant notoriety that he was giving to the quiet Nazareth household. Sometimes a man's "friends" make apology for him by the explanation that he is a little "off" and should be excused. Few preachers of energy and individuality escape such "friends."

12. *Understanding Children.*—But if Jesus was misunderstood by others, he himself was at one with little children. They are the severest critics of all, for they have no affectations and either like you or do not like you. If a preacher can win and hold the children, he need not bother about the older people. They will at least be sure to understand his sermons if the children do so. Most of them will love the preacher because he has won their children. It seems odd to us today that the world has been so slow in appreciating childhood, which is the real wealth of a nation. Children were never in the way of Jesus. Even the apostles once rebuked a group of mothers for bringing their little children to Jesus to receive his blessing (10:13). They evidently felt that it was a bother to Jesus to be interrupted by children, much as some people dislike to have children in church, and, as a result, they are not there when older.

Today after almost any Sunday school service one sees a great crowd of the pupils going home instead of to church. But Jesus was indignant at the disciples for such an estimate of his attitude toward children, urged that children be allowed to come to him, made a little child the example of the subjects of the kingdom, and took the children into his arms and blessed them (10:14–16). Once before Jesus took a little child into his arms and set him in the midst of the disciples as an object lesson to them in their disputes, a sort of kindergarten lesson for the preachers. Jesus has created the modern child's world of joy and gladness and always has had room in his heart and in his arms for them.

13. *The Test of the Greatest Preacher.*—People differ greatly in their views of preaching, and that is not wholly bad, for the great variety of preachers suits different classes. No one preacher pleases all. John the Baptist did not please everyone, nor did Jesus or Paul. There is no one single test of good speaking, but there is a test for the greatness of a preacher's ministry. The sermon is by no means all of his work, important as that is. Preachers are sometimes jealous of each other as doctors are envious of doctors, lawyers of lawyers. Even the twelve apostles "disputed one with another on the way, who was the greatest" (9:34).

Now, the ambition to be great is not in itself evil any more than is the longing to be good. It all depends on one's notion of greatness. If it is simply self-aggrandizement, then it is vanity. If it is self-advancement at the expense of others, it is evil. Jesus gave the disciples a new ideal of greatness, that of humility and service. "If any man would be first, he shall be last of all, and servant of all" (9:35). This is an absolutely revolutionary idea, and yet it is destined to conquer the world in the end. It lies at the root of real patriotism, of love of father and mother and child, of all the Christian activities of the world, of missions, of Red

Cross work, of the preacher's whole life, of the life of every child of God.

14. *The Ministry of Sympathy.*—In it all Christ never lost the sympathetic chord that gives nobility to human effort. Compassed on every side by theological obscurantism and ecclesiastical red tape, Jesus burst through it all. On his way to the crucifixion he bore his own cross like the Son of man and like the Son of God. Even on the cross Jesus prayed for forgiveness for those who were taking his life. Tragedy enters into the lives of other preachers, though not on this scale. Broadus used to say that sympathy was the chief element in effective preaching. But no preacher is really efficient until his heart is touched with sorrows. Then he will know how to be a sympathetic and tender shepherd to the lambs that are lost in the storm, and he will go after them and bring them back. It was the cry of the lost sheep that broke the heart of Christ. They are still crying on the mountains for you and me.

15. *Courage unto Death.*—No man ever displayed more courage than Jesus. The minister is lost who is a coward. The people will not respect him or hear his message. Criticism is to be expected by those who bring a new message and who attack vested interests and inherited prejudices and established traditions. Jesus, from the standpoint of the Pharisees, was an iconoclast and a dangerous revolutionist whose work was subversive of all the religious traditions of the fathers. He early made his choice and attacked the current religious leaders who were responsible for the shackles on the people and defied them. He did this boldly and repeatedly when he saw that this course led to the cross. He claimed power to forgive sins when the Pharisees accused him of blasphemy and healed the paralytic to prove the truth of his claim (2:10). Jesus disregarded pharisaic exclusiveness and associated with the publicans

and sinners at Levi's feast (2:16). He justified his disciples' disregard of the stated fasts of the Jews, to the disgust of the disciples of John now in collusion with the disciples of the Pharisees. This he did on the ground of the radical difference between Christianity and current Judaism. He defied pharisaic rules about sabbath observance and justified his right to interpret the day as the servant, not the master of man (2:23 to 3:6).

One of the sharpest attacks made against Christ by the Pharisees was because his disciples ignored their scruples by eating with unwashed hands (7:1–23). Jesus charged them with setting at naught the word of God by the traditions of men. Jesus was a religious and social reformer, and he struck hard at the abuses in his time. He hit hardest the professional pietists of the day whom he termed hypocrites because they stood in the way of the establishment of real righteousness. Vital religion was hindered by the dead ceremonialism all about him. Every evangelist feels the chill of a cold church life when he meets it.

Jesus moved as Master everywhere, whether in the midst of hostile criticism from Pharisees and home folks (3:20–35); or pressed by a curious and superficial crowd by the sea who did not know how to use their eyes and their ears and their minds, and to whom the parabolic teaching was a closed book (4:1–9); or with his own disciples who struggled to apprehend his enigmatic sayings (4:10–34) and hopelessly floundered in doubt when they seemed to be sinking in the storm at sea (4:35–41); or grappling with a legion of demons who went from man to swine in a mad rush to the sea, with the result that Jesus was urged to leave that region (5:1–20); or feeling power go out of him as a poor woman touched the hem of his garment in the throng (5:30); or overcoming death in the home of Jairus when he took the little girl by the hand and lifted her up to the amazement of all (5:41); or once more astonishing the people of Nazareth by his words and his wonders since they could not comprehend how a man reared in their town could really do what Jesus did (6:3). It has often been a mystery to people how a green boy reared among them could ever come to be a master workman for God. We are all provincial in our prejudices.

16. *An Itinerant Preacher.*—Jesus was constantly on the go during his brief ministry. He went on to "the next towns" (1:38), like the modern missionary evangelist. There was little time for study in the modern sense of that term. We do not think of Jesus as a bookish preacher, and yet his preaching astonished the people precisely by marvelous insight into the meaning of the Old Testament Scriptures. He denounced the rabbis (the current preachers) for their slavery to tradition and ignorance of the Word of God. "Ye leave the commandment of God, and hold fast the tradition of men, . . . making void the word of God by your tradition" (7:8–13). Some scholars think that Jesus was a student of the Jewish apocalypses and that the teaching of Jesus reveals an acquaintance with several of the noncanonical Jewish writings. Be that as it may, the most striking thing about the teaching of Jesus is its originality and its universality.

The thinking of Jesus is modern and still far ahead of the best modern ideals in spite of its Palestinian environment. Isolated sayings of Jesus have parallels in the Talmud, but the Talmud is intellectually dead, while the words of Jesus have life and power to rejuvenate the world. The modern man's deepest philosophy is following after this itinerant Galilean preacher.

Preachers today often excuse themselves from profound study on the plea that they are too busy. The manifold demands of a city pastorate preclude technical biblical knowledge. And yet no sermons through the ages are comparable in pith and power with those of this busiest of all preachers whom the crowds pressed almost to suffocation. These sermons dropped from his lips in matchless perfection of substance and form. Unwasted though Jesus was, eternal Youth that he is, yet the multitudes sapped his vital energy as he felt power go out from him (5:30). Anyone who has really preached knows what it is to be "clean gone." There can be no effective preaching without expenditure of vital force.

17. *Christ's Method and Manner in Preaching.*—Jesus used the conversational style as a rule. He spoke over nobody's head. Sometimes in the presence of great multitudes he spoke in an elevated tone of voice so as to be heard. "And he called to him the multitude again, and said unto them, Hear me all of you, and understand" (7:14). Every speaker knows what this means. Mere loudness will not carry conviction, but in the presence of a great crowd one must make himself heard if possible so as to drive the truth home. But often Jesus spoke as the teacher to a smaller group gathered round him. In this free interplay we see Jesus in his usual conversational mood.

It is a curious instance of development that our word "homiletics" comes from the Greek *homileo,* which means to converse. Luke uses it of the talk of the two disciples on the way to Emmaus as "they communed with each other." Jesus was quick to notice inattention and often urged closer attention. "If any man hath ears to hear, let him hear" (4:23). He was responsive to the changing moods of his audience, as every orator is. Jesus not only had compassion on the multitude and "began to teach them" (6:34), eager as they were for the bread of life, but he also knew when to stop and to send the multitude away, even when they did not wish to go (6:45). He had compassion for their physical wants also (8:2); "They will faint on the way; and some of them are come from far." The modern preacher who is utterly oblivious to the physical conditions of his ministry will fail to win a hearing and will lose his crowd.

Mark has the advantage of Peter's keen eyes and tells us much about the looks and gestures of Jesus. "And when he had looked round about on them with anger, being grieved at the hardening of their heart, he saith unto the man, Stretch forth thy hand" (3:5). One can almost see the flash of the eye as Jesus swept round the synagogue that look of scorn that set the Pharisees and Herodians wild with rage. When his mother and brothers came to take Jesus home, "looking round on them that sat round about him, he saith, Behold, my mother and my brethren" (3:34). When the rich young ruler came to Jesus he "looking upon him loved him" (10:21). "And Jesus looked round about, and saith" (10:23); "Jesus looking upon them saith" (10:27). Mark gives this vivid picture of the strain written on the face of Jesus: "And Jesus was going before them: and they were amazed; and they that followed were afraid" (10:32).

It is easy to see in Mark that Jesus used rapartee, wit, humor, irony, sarcasm, invective, question, appeal, rebuke. It was all life where Jesus was. He let his hearers talk back. The electric spark flashed and struck fire. It is not necessary to think that Jesus was a student of Greek rhetoric or of the rabbinical dialectic. But it is not hard to find examples of the diatribe, of the Socratic method of questioning, of the rabbinical refinement of thought. What we find in Christ's teaching and preaching is not the rules of the schools or of the books but the appeal to the laws of human thought. We are in the presence of One who is master of the mind of man and plays upon it with the precision of a master musician. Jesus encouraged questions. The people asked him why, what, and how. But he often gave question for question, as in 2:18 f. and in 2:24 f.

Often Jesus would challenge attention at the start by a question, as in 3:4. People learned to expect something when he put out these sharp questions. An example of irony is in 7:9: "Full well do ye reject the commandment of God, that ye may keep your tradition." It is jejune not to see the point here. The playful wit of Jesus appears in his bantering repartee with the Syrophenician woman, who brightly took up the word of Christ about the dogs: "Yea, Lord; even the dogs under the table eat of the children's crumbs" (7:28). "For this saying go thy way." Did not Jesus smile graciously upon her as he spoke? Sometimes Jesus has to rebuke his own disciples even sharply, as in 7:18: "Are ye so without understanding also?" Even to Peter he had once to say, "Get thee behind me, Satan" (8:33). To James and John, Christ had to reply, "Ye know not what ye ask" (10:38).

Jesus met current problems in his preaching, but only to show the eternal value of spiritual realities. In an unspiritual age he struck the spiritual note and held to it, though his own disciples failed to understand his conception of the kingdom even after his resurrection (Acts 1:6). His own age crucified him because he would not fall in with the current theology of the rabbis. They killed the Prince of life, who brought life and immortality to light.

The illustrations of Jesus surpass those of all other preachers. The rabbis used parables before Jesus taught. We have many of them in the Talmud, but they do not measure up to the standards set by Jesus. Even the disciples were puzzled by the parables of Christ and asked him in private to interpret them (4:10–34). They served various purposes. They caught flagging attention and held it by the power of the story. They sent a shaft where the truth could else not go. They concealed the message from those not able and not worthy to hear it, while revealing to the spiritually minded the mystery of the kingdom (4:11). The point of the story would stick with the parable and be understood later if not at the moment. Christ's parables are the perfection of storytelling and linger in the mind with the charm of sweet music or lash the conscience like whips. The parables of Jesus always illustrate. But this subject calls for special treatment in the next chapter.

VIII

The Parables of Jesus
in Mark's Gospel

He taught them many things in parables.

MARK 4:2.

1. *Parables Less Prominent than Miracles in Mark.*—
Mark's Gospel is noted for its report of miracles rather than
its record of parables. The deeds of Jesus rather than his
words confront us. And yet the teaching of Christ is by no
means neglected. It is here alone that Jesus' command,
"Believe in the gospel" (Mark 1:15) is preserved. Papias
expressly says that Mark "wrote accurately what he recalled
of the things said or done by Christ," what he recalled of
Peter's preaching about Jesus. In a word, in Mark's Gospel
we see Christ in action, but "Jesus came into Galilee, preaching the gospel of God" (1:14). Jesus in the Second Gospel
is not a mere miracle worker. He is distinctly and at once
set forth as the preacher and teacher. In the synagogue in
Capernaum "they were astonished at his teaching: for he
taught them as having authority, and not as the scribes"
(1:22). The teaching of Jesus was as sensational as his
miracles. "And they were all amazed, insomuch that they
questioned among themselves, saying, What is this? a new
teaching!" (1:27).

2. *Definition of Parable.*—No element of Christ's teaching was more bewildering to his hearers than his use of parables. The Jewish rabbis made copious use of parables, but they lack the stamp of originality that belongs to those of Jesus. The parables of the rabbis, as we have them in the Talmud, are more or less perfunctory and commonplace, not to say artificial, unnatural, and fantastic. They do not haunt the mind and linger in the memory in the way that those of Jesus do.

The beauty of his parables charms us even when we do not at once see the point of the story. As a rule the point is clear, but sometimes it is purposely obscure for the confusion of the enemies of Christ. An illustration is designed to throw light on the point under discussion. The parable is one form of illustration. It takes a familiar fact in nature and puts it beside the less familiar moral or spiritual truth. The comparison clarifies the truth. The parable may be extended narrative or crisp epigrammatic metaphor. It may be formal comparison or implied comparison. It is unlike the fable which is grotesque and contrary to nature. The parable, while either fiction or fact, is always in harmony with nature. It is always possible and true to the laws of the person or thing used for the story. The parable could have happened.

It is not always easy to draw the line between parable and metaphor. Jesus "saw Simon and Andrew casting a net in the sea; for they were fishers. And Jesus said unto them, Come ye after me, and I will take you to become fishers of men" (Mark 1:16 f.). Put beside this passage these words from Luke 4:23: "And he said unto them, Doubtless ye will say unto me this parable, Physician, heal thyself: whatsoever we have heard done at Capernaum, do also here in thine own country." The parabolic proverb lies in the use of "physician." Why not call "fishers of men" a parable? Must we not, then, find a parabolic proverb also in Mark 2:17: "They that are whole have no need of a physician, but they that are sick: I came not to call the righteous, but sinners"?

Jesus here first states the parable and then explains it. How far to use details in explaining the parable is always a question.

3. *Groups of Parables.*—So in Mark 2:18–22 Jesus employed three parables in defense of his disciples who had not joined in one of the stated fasts of the Jews with John's disciples and the disciples of the Pharisees when they united in complaint against them. One regrets to see the disciples of the Baptist thus drawn into opposition to Jesus by the activity of the Pharisees. But clearly Jesus had gone further in his independent attitude toward Jewish ceremonialism than John. Besides, John was still in prison and his disciples may have resented the apparent indifference of Jesus to the fate of his forerunner. Already disciples of John had exhibited jealousy of the growing fame of Jesus (John 3:26).

The disciples of Jesus had just gone with him to the feast of Levi with the publicans and sinners (Mark 2:13–17), probably at the very time of one of the regular fasts (Mark 2:18), hence the reaction of John's disciples to the side of the Pharisees, the critics of Jesus. In defense Jesus used his favorite method of parabolic teaching. He contrasted the inevitable conflict between the old and the new by the parables of the sons of the bridal chamber (companions of the bridegroom), the patched garment, and the wineskins. Mark does not call these sayings parables, but Luke does: "And he spake also a parable unto them" (5:36). Luke then gives the parable of the patched garment. If one is a parable, the others are.

It is interesting to note that the Baptist had termed Jesus

97

"the bridegroom" and himself "the friend of the bride-groom" (John 3:29). There is thus an echo of the Baptist's own words in the reply of Jesus to the mistaken disciples of John. They are in the wrong group and have missed their way about both John and Jesus. These three parables present in wonderful fashion the line of cleavage between Jewish ceremonialism and spiritual Christianity. The gospel of Christ is not to be cribbed and cabined by the rites and ceremonies of the old dispensation which had their place and service then. Matthew and Luke give these three parables, but they evidently get them from Mark who wrote first and records Peter's vivid recital of the words of Jesus. Christianity is still bursting the shell of the old as the life of the new expands.

The miracles of Jesus are acted parables, and the parables are pedagogic miracles, as Augustine said. In Mark 5:39 Jesus, upon entering the house of Jairus where many were weeping and wailing greatly, says, "Why make ye a tumult, and weep? the child is not dead, but sleepeth." It is probable that here Jesus is using figurative language as in John 11:4: "This sickness is not unto death," and in 11:11: "Our friend Lazarus is fallen asleep; but I go, that I may awake him out of sleep." And yet Lazarus had been dead for four days when Jesus raised him. But even so, the language is more metaphorical than technically parabolic.

But there is no doubt about the parables in Mark 3:23–27, for Mark expressly says, "And he called them unto him, and said unto them in parables." Then we have several brief pictures about Satan casting out Satan, a kingdom divided against itself, a house divided against itself—all like cinema flashes that swiftly turn on the light and show the utter absurdity of the charge that Jesus was casting out demons by the power of Beelzebub. Jesus often used this rapid-fire method with a number of parables, for instance, the three in Luke 14, the three in Luke 15 (the lost sheep, the lost coin, the lost son), the seven and more in Matthew 13, and the three in Matthew 21 and 22. Each parable presents a new facet of the truth while all sides of the question are brought to light.

Another group of parables occurs in Mark 4:2–34. Mark states in so many words that "he taught them many things in parables," evidently meaning that there were many more on this occasion besides those that he records. After giving several (the sower, the lamp, the seed growing of itself, the grain of mustard seed) he adds this striking comment: "And with many such parables spake he the word unto them, as they were able to hear it; and without a parable spake he not unto them" (4:33 f.). Matthew 13 records nine on the same day, counting the lamp and the householder as being parables, as they manifestly are.

Mark does not mean to say that Jesus always confined himself to parables but that on this day (the busy day, the day of the blasphemous accusation) he did so purposely. The disciples were greatly puzzled over the number and the length of these narrative parables. "And when he was alone, they that were about him with the twelve asked of him the parables" (4:10). They wanted to know why he used them and what he meant by them. The reply of Jesus shows that on this day he was employing parables as a means of concealing truth from those who would treat it as pearls cast before swine and yet at the same time as a blessing for those with eyes to see. "Unto you is given the mystery of the kingdom of God: but unto them that are without, all things are done in parables: that seeing they may see, and not perceive; and hearing they may hear, and not understand; lest haply they should turn again, and it should be forgiven them" (4:11 f.).

This is a hard saying and sounds unsympathetic, but we

must remember that Jesus had in mind those who had just accused him of being in league with Satan and whom he had denounced as guilty of the unpardonable sin in attributing to the devil the manifest works of the Spirit of God. They deserved this judgment of obscurity for this heinous sin. The parables thus used were a pillar of light to the spiritually minded and a pillar of darkness to the adversaries of Jesus. Jesus wished people to understand him if they were kindly disposed toward him. So he proceeded to explain the parable of the sower with minute detail. "Know ye not this parable? and how shall ye know all the parables?" (4:13). "But privately to his own disciples he expounded all things" (4:34).

Thus we see the Master giving his disciples private interpretation of this aspect of his public teaching. They were to know the mystery of the kingdom. It was no longer a hidden secret to them but a blessed secret that was revealed. "For there is nothing hid, save that it should be manifested; neither was anything made secret, but that it should come to light" (4:22). Christ did not change the primary purpose of parables in thus employing them as a curse upon his obdurate enemies. He put the lamp upon the lampstand, not under the bushel, that it may give light for those with eyes to see. The blind do not see. The wilfully deaf do not hear. "If any man hath ears to hear, let him hear." Jesus thus made direct appeal for attention and pointed his words with these arrows of conviction. He knew only too well how volatile some of them were, how preoccupied others were, how hardhearted many were, how few really would let the seed bear fruit in heart and life.

Other teachers come after the King. If Jesus found it so difficult to win attention, to hold it, to plant the seed of truth where it would find responsive soil, we need not wonder at our frequent failures in teaching and preaching.

The very parables of Jesus that charmed so many threw others into utter confusion of thought. But Jesus was willing to cast bread upon the water in hope that it would come back after many days. The stories of Jesus stick in the mind like burs. Some day the point of the story will be plain. He knew that when he told the parable. Peter, like the rest, was greatly impressed by the parables of that busy day. They stirred the disciples to talk and to learn.

It has been said that only narrative parables required explanation, for similitudes and illustrative instances carried their own meaning. So they did, but the hearers by no means always saw it. The parable of the sower is really allegory, while that of the growing seed is similitude.

4. *Difficulty in Understanding Christ's Parables.*—Jesus was a prophet, and so it is hardly necessary to call the proverb in Mark 6:4 a parable: "A prophet is not without honor, save in his own country, and among his own kin, and in his own house." It is a parabolic proverb like that in Luke 6:39 which is called a parable: "Can the blind guide the blind?" The dullness of the disciples in comprehending some of the simplest parables of Jesus is due to their theological prepossessions. Their pharisaic environment colored their vision so that it was hard for them to see the obvious (to us) spiritual truth.

In the clash with the Pharisees over the tradition of washing the hands for ceremonial purity Jesus said, "Hear me all of you, and understand: there is nothing from without the man, that going into him can defile him; but the things which proceed out of the man are those that defile the man" (Mark 7:14 f.). Then Jesus made a special plea for attention, and the parable is so very obvious that we almost fail to see the parabolic form. And yet, "when he was entered into the house from the multitude, his disciples asked of him the parable" (Mark 7:17). They actually could not see the inevitable implication of Christ's teaching concerning the uselessness of the pharisaic rites. Matthew reports that the disciples said, "Knowest thou that the Pharisees were offended, when they heard this saying?" (15:12). The disciples evidently felt that Jesus had gone too far in his criticism of the Pharisees, and they did not know precisely where they stood themselves.

One has only to recall Peter's difficulty later in Joppa in understanding the vision on the housetop when he refused the Lord's invitation to rise, slay, and eat. "Not so, Lord; for I have never eaten anything that is common and unclean" (Acts 10:14). That was after the bestowal of the Holy Spirit at Pentecost.

Then in this incident in the Gospels, "Peter answered and said unto him, Declare unto us the parable" (Matt. 15:15). Peter spoke for all of them who realized that they could not go with Jesus in his breach with pharisaism on this point, if they understood his parable. So they begged for further light. Jesus sharply upbraided their dulness: "Are ye so without understanding also? Perceive ye not, that whatsoever from without goeth into the man, it cannot defile him; because it goeth not into his heart, but into his belly, and goeth out into the draught?" (Mark 7:18). Mark does not give the reply of the disciples, if they made any, which is hardly likely.

As we have seen, Peter did not see the bearing of this parable until his experience at Joppa and Caesarea (Acts 10). But Mark breaks right into the explanation of Jesus (7:18-23) by a sharp anacoluthon at the close of verse 19, "making all meats clean." This is probably due to a side remark of Peter as he recounted the incident and to Mark's preservation of this touch of life. Peter's explanatory comment reflects the new light on this parable that he obtained at Joppa.

In the intellectual passage of arms between Jesus and the Syrophenician woman (Mark 7:25–30) Jesus said, "Let the children first be filled: for it is not meet to take the children's bread and cast it to the dogs." This proverb might have cut the woman to the quick, Greek as she was. But instead of flying off the handle at the apparent rebuff, with nimble wit she caught up the parable of Jesus and gave it a deft turn to her own advantage: "Yea, Lord; e en the dogs [the little dogs, literally] under the table eat of the children's crumbs." It was bright and it was true, and she scored by her neat and complete answer. Jesus said in reply, "For this saying go thy way; the demon is gone out of thy daughter." Jesus rewarded her bright faith. Is it irreverent to imagine a merry twinkle in the eyes of Jesus as the woman showed her gratitude and joy? Humor and pathos lie close together, as this incident shows. The woman's courage carried her through, and she took Christ at his word and went home to her daughter. In the presence of so much stupidity in spiritual things Jesus seemed to find positive delight in the quick wit of this Greek woman.

Quite otherwise was the dreary dulness of the disciples concerning "the leaven of the Pharisees and the leaven of Herod" (Mark 8:15). The literalness of the disciples in trying to apply the warning of the master is absolutely jejune when "they reasoned one with another, saying, We have no bread." They thought the warning against the kind of bread used by the Pharisees and Herod needless because they had no bread at all. To be sure, the disciples were not always so dull as this, else they would have been hopeless pupils. The best of us are duller at times than is usual for us. But the incapacity of the disciples on this occasion greatly disappointed Jesus.

His sharp questions are more than justified by their slowness to grasp this simple parable: "Why reason ye, because ye have no bread? do ye not yet perceive, neither understand? have ye your heart hardened? Having eyes, see ye not? and having ears, hear ye not? and do ye not remember?" (8:17 f.). Then Jesus reminded them of the feeding of the five thousand and of the four thousand, acted parables as these miracles were. Once more the Master asks, "Do ye not yet understand?" (8:21). There Mark leaves the incident, striking testimony to the fidelity of Peter in reporting his own obtuseness. Matthew, however, states that after Christ's repeated questions "then understood they that he bade them not beware of the leaven of bread, but of the teaching of the Pharisees and Sadducees" (16:12). Jesus was the most patient of teachers and had given the disciples parable upon parable. They were without excuse and without resource, though at last they saw the point. The true teacher will keep at it until he makes the dull ones see what he means. The parable is designed to turn on the light, but here light had to be thrust on the parable.

5. *Pointedness of Christ's Parables.*—Is it not a parable when Jesus rebuked Peter by saying, "Get thee behind me, Satan; for thou mindest not the things of God, but the things of men" (Mark 8:33)? Certainly this sudden and sharp epithet shocked Peter and the others and ought to have opened their eyes to the real meaning of Jesus concerning his death. If Mark obtained the account of this incident from Peter, Peter did not refrain from showing how he had distressed the heart of Christ.

Mark speaks of a group of parables in 12:1: "And he began to speak unto them in parables." He gives, however, only one, that of the householder who let his vineyard out to husbandmen who abused their trust and finally killed the householder's son. By this parable Jesus portrayed the treatment that he was receiving at the hands of the Jews. It was part of his defense to the Sanhedrin when they attacked him in the Temple on the last day of his public ministry. There is a threat in the application of the parable concerning God's judgment on the Jews for their mistreatment of his Son: "What therefore will the lord of the vineyard do? he will come and destroy the husbandmen, and will give the vineyard unto others" (12:9). The Jewish leaders saw the point of this parable, which went home like a sure arrow: "And they sought to lay hold on him; and they feared the multitude; for they perceived that he spake the parable against them: and they left him, and went away" (12:12). The anger, fear, and vacillation of the Sanhedrin come out finely in this summary by Mark. Matthew narrates two other parables on this same occasion, that of the two sons and that of the marriage feast and the wedding garment. They helped to clinch the point of the fate of the Jews for rejecting the Son of God.

Once more in Mark 13:28 we find a parable: "Now from the fig tree learn her parable." Jesus used the tender branches of the fig tree as the sign of summer. There the disciples were to watch for the signs of the coming doom of Jerusalem and also for the coming of the Son of man at the end. It is possible that in verses 30 and 31 Christ referred to the destruction of Jerusalem: "This generation shall not pass away, until all these things be accomplished." In verse 32 we may have the further and more remote event of his second coming: "But of that day or that hour knoweth no one, not even the angels in heaven, neither the Son, but the Father." In this interpretation Jesus is not contradicting himself but has in mind two events, one a symbol of the other. If this view is correct, the new paragraph should begin with verse 32. So the Master proceeds, "Take ye heed, watch and pray: for ye know not when the time is" (13:33). Then Christ gave the parable of the porter and the other servants to illustrate the great need for watching for his coming (13:34–37). The master of the house in his absence gave each servant his task and commanded the porter also to watch for his coming. The sudden return of the lord of the house would be very embarrassing if all the servants were sleeping. Alas, how dull we have all become and how little we really "watch" for the Lord's coming.

Shall we call the use of the fruit of the vine for the blood of Christ and the bread for his body a parable? When Jesus said, "This is my body" and "This is my blood of the covenant, which is poured out for many" (14:22, 24), he was not using language literally as the Roman Catholics hold. It is a figurative and symbolic use and can be properly termed a parable.

6. *Summary.*—We may now gather up the facts in Mark's report of Christ's parables. There are twenty-two in the list above, but that is giving a generous latitude to the use of the word. Several are barely more than metaphors. A number are proverbs. Most of them are very brief. In fact, there are only two of any length, the sower in chapter 4 and the householder and the vineyard in chapter 12. This is quite in contrast to Luke and Matthew, which have a number of parables of considerable length (Luke 14, 15, 16, 18 and Matthew 13, 21, 22, 25). The count of the number of parables spoken by Jesus ranges all the way from twenty-seven to fifty-nine. Mark has few of the great kingdom parables found in Matthew and Luke, though one of them, the seed growing of itself, occurs only in Mark. In Mark the parables of Jesus are like momentary flashlights, a sort of touch-and-go in the teaching of Jesus. He used parables "as they were able to hear it" (4:33). And yet Mark several times alludes to the great number of Christ's parables. The great majority of his parables were probably like those in Mark, vivid and sharp. The great number of them seem like the constant play of lightning in the storm and darkness.

IX

The Teaching of Jesus
in Mark's Gospel

*They were all amazed, insomuch that they ques-
tioned among themselves, saying, What is this? a
new teaching!*   MARK 1:27.

1. *The Objectivity of Mark.*—We do not usually look to
Mark's Gospel for the teaching of Jesus but rather to Matthew, Luke, and John. In fact, it is now almost a commonplace in New Testament criticism that Mark and Q (the
Logia of Jesus) are the two main sources of Matthew and
Luke. Bacon is quite sure that the canonical Mark is em-
bellished at points by the use of Q.

However that may be, there is an undoubted contrast
between the objectivity of Mark's narrative and the discourses in the other Gospels.

Neither Matthew nor Luke considers his task performed
without embodying the substance of the sayings or teaching of the Lord. Matthew in particular regards it as the
very essence of an evangelist's duty to teach men to observe
all things whatsoever Jesus had commanded. Mark certainly
was not ignorant of such teaching or commandments of the
Lord, even if we refuse his acquaintance with the particular
document employed by Matthew and Luke. Yet he leaves his
readers without information on the law of Jesus.

We may admit that Mark was familiar with Q. He avoided using Q because that was already in use precisely as the Fourth Gospel mainly supplements the Synoptic Gospels. There are scholars, however, who deny that Mark made any use of Q. Others argue that Mark has no dogmatic purpose and writes with simple objectivity. And yet it will not do to say that Mark has no purpose and no plan in his Gospel. His purpose is simply to produce belief in the person of Jesus as Son of God. In Mark's Gospel Jesus is presented as a herald of the kingdom, then as a teacher with the note of authority, then as a prophet, then as a miracle worker, the Son of man, and finally as the Messiah, the Son of God. Thus the plan of Mark begins to appear. Jesus does not lay down a program of the messianic kingdom by means of argued discourse. Rather, the principles regulating his activity are slowly evolved by the events of his life. Mark's Gospel proves the deity of Jesus mainly by the force of the work which he did. Mark has grouped his material for a purpose. He wishes to show by means of events in the life of Jesus how the teaching of the Lord took on substance and shape in the face of sharp, clearly defined opposition.

2. *A Minimum of Teaching.*—There is in Mark a minimum of teaching by Christ, but the teaching is present and is worth our study. Jesus is repeatedly called "teacher" (4:38; 5:35; 9:17, 38; 12:14; 13:1). Bacon in his *Beginnings of the Gospel Story* thinks that in Mark 8:27 to 10:52 we at last find Mark giving the content of Jesus' message. He refers to this material on the doctrine of the cross as Mark's "Sermon on the Mount." He attributes this portion of Mark to Paul's influence: "The Paulinism of Mark is supremely manifest in this evangelist's whole conception of what constitutes the apostolic message." Pfleiderer goes so far as to charge Mark with inventing these "Pauline" speeches and

attributing them to Jesus. "The pupil of Paul is most evident in the speeches, which the evangelist did not find in his source-book or in the Palestinian tradition, but created independently and for the first time fitted into the traditional material as the leading religious motives for the judgment of the history of Jesus." He assumes that Mark is partly responsible for theologizing the Jesus of history into the Christ of Paul. It is quite to the point, therefore, since a purpose like that is attributed to Mark, to see what he really does represent Jesus as teaching.

3. *The Method of Mark.*—The headline properly describes the book. It is "the beginning of the gospel of Jesus Christ, the Son of God." But it is the method of Jesus with which we are here concerned, not that of the Gospel. It should be pointed out that the method which we find in the Gospel of Mark bears all the appearance of being the method of Jesus himself. Mark has not imposed his own method on the materials which he received; those materials themselves reflect the method of the master Teacher. He does not engage in extended discourse; he meets questions as they arise. But the answers to those questions anticipate the problems faced by the later church. This is the method of Jesus in his teaching. He seized the occasions as they came to proclaim the message of the kingdom, now on this point, now on that. But the teaching of Jesus is coherent and consistent in spite of its incidental occasion and aphoristic form. One has only to think of Socrates as reported by Plato and Xenophon to see how this can be true. Let us then turn to the sayings of Jesus in Mark and see what they teach us.

4. *Logia of Jesus.*—The first logion of Jesus is in 1:15 and reminds us of the message of the Baptist in 1:4. Like John, the Master announced the fulness of the time and the nearness of the kingdom of God. We are not told what the word

"kingdom" means in the mouth of Jesus, but the event shows that Jesus conceived it to be a spiritual reign in men's hearts, not the political rule looked for by the Pharisees. The duty of repentance was urged, a turning of the heart and life to God. Faith in the gospel was commended. Jesus had a definite message (the gospel) or good news, and he expected men to believe it. This saying of Jesus is the theme of the Galilean ministry.

The next logion of Jesus is in 1:17. It is the call to Simon and Andrew to follow Jesus permanently, with the promise of making them "fishers of men," the only really big business in the world. The call caught the hearts of these two enterprising laymen and also won James and John, who left their business to go into the bigger task of winning men to Christ. The message of Jesus thus has point and force. It is public and personal. Jesus won these four followers by direct personal appeal. He claimed them, and they acknowledged his authority. He drafted them for service.

The next logion is in 1:25, spoken to the demon which Jesus commanded to come out of the poor man. Jesus here recognized the reality of demon possession and exercised his power over the evil spirit. The demon had addressed Jesus as "the Holy One of God," but Jesus commanded him to be silent, not wishing testimony from such a source. The demoniacs seemed to know that Jesus was the Son of God and loudly proclaimed it (cf. 5:7 f.).

The next saying is in 1:38 and concerns the purpose of Jesus to leave the crowds in Capernaum and push on to the next towns. Only one more incident comes in chapter 1, the healing of the leper, to whose pitiful appeal Jesus said, "I will; be thou made clean" (1:41) and then told the man to go and show himself to the priest (1:44). But these logia reveal Jesus as Lord and Master of men, as teacher and prophet, whose words and deeds had set Galilee ablaze.

5. *Making a Point of the Teaching.*—In chapter 2 the teaching is more prominent. In fact, Jesus forgave the sins of the paralytic before he healed him, and when challenged, he asserted his power to forgive sins and his consequent equality with God and proceeded to heal the man in order to prove that he possessed the right to forgive sins (2:5–11). This incident illustrates well how the teaching of Jesus in Mark's Gospel is associated with the actual events. The profoundest sayings of Christ burst forth spontaneously out of the everyday work. Here Jesus revealed a consciousness of his equality with God quite Johannine in tone, and that was considered blasphemy by the scribes present. The use of the phrase "the Son of man" is also characteristic. It is messianic in fact without giving his enemies a technical ground for arresting him. It also puts Jesus, though the Son of God, as the Father called him and as the demon understood (1:24; 5:7), on a level with men in sympathy and love as their representative and ideal.

In 2:17 we have one of the crisp parables of Jesus that throw a flood of light on himself and his enemies. The Pharisees posed as righteous and called other men sinners, as we know from the Psalms of the Pharisees. "Righteous" and "sinners" are here, then, class distinctions. Jesus does not mean to admit that the Pharisees are really righteous but only that their claim to that class reflects their complaint at him for preaching to, and eating with, the publicans and sinners. It is a neat turn of unanswerable wit and is a complete justification for Christianity's mission to the so-called sinful classes. As a matter of fact, pharisaic pride (cf. Matt. 6) is one of the worst and most hopeless of sins.

In 2:19–22 Jesus is again on the defensive and justifies the conduct of his disciples in abstaining from one of the stated fasts which the disciples of John and the Pharisees were observing (2:18). The three parables (the bridegroom, the undressed cloth, the wineskins) all show how radically Christianity differs from current Judaism (the pharisaic orthodoxy). Jesus made it plain that Christianity has burst the swaddling clothes of Jewish ceremonialism and can never again be put back into such bonds. And yet various types of Christianity have tried to put clamps upon the life of the spiritual man. Jesus here attacks sacramentarianism as a system, while commending fasting when it is the natural expression of real grief and not mere custom or display. Jesus also revealed foreknowledge of his approaching death and showed a messianic consciousness, calling himself "the bridegroom."

Few things irritated the Pharisees more than Christ's failure to observe their rules for sabbath observance. His defense against their attack made them more angry than ever by reason of his claim of superiority to these rules, and even to the day itself, as the Son of man. Indeed he asserted that the day was for man's blessing, not for his injury (2:27 f.). Jesus challenged the pharisaic punctiliousness concerning the sabbath as slavery to the letter and refusal to do good and willingness to let men die on that day (3:1). This attitude of Jesus widened the breach between him and the Pharisees and healed that between them and the Herodians, who joined hands plotting his death (3:5 f.).

In 3:22–30 Jesus not only defended himself against the charge of being in league with the devil by a series of brief parables but also attacked the Pharisees with tremendous force and showed that they were guilty of an eternal sin which has no forgiveness, since they attributed to the devil the manifest work of the Holy Spirit. Jesus here denied universal salvation and proclaimed eternal punishment for some. In sharp contrast with this incident, note the beautiful words of Jesus in 3:34 f. when he found his mother and his brethren among those who do the will of God. This he said at the time when his own family supposed that he was beside himself and had come to take him home.

Chapter 4 is the parable chapter in Mark. We have only a few specimens of the many parables spoken on that day (4:2, 10, 33 f.). The parable of the sower is given and explained by Jesus and shows the variety of hearers who hear the word that is spoken, as every preacher finds out to his sorrow. The place for the lamp is on the stand so as to give light. How careless men are with their opportunities. The mysterious growth of the kingdom in the heart is illustrated by the story of the growing seed. The expanding power of the kingdom is shown by the mustard seed's development.

And yet with all the care in Christ's teaching the disciples were still fearful and timid in their faith when caught in the storm. The power of Christ over wind and wave amazed them (4:41), which shows that only gradually were they grasping the truth about Christ's person and mission. In 5:19 Jesus told the former demoniac to go home and tell his friends what great things God had done for him, whereas he told the leper not to tell anyone (1:44). But this was in Gentile territory where there was no danger of undue excitement, especially as Jesus was leaving the region. In Nazareth, Jesus revealed the fact that he knew how unable the people in his home town were to appreciate him at his real worth (6:4). The directions that Jesus gave the twelve for the Galilean tour were particular and special and not meant to apply to all mission campaigns (6:7–11).

The feeding of the five thousand was the occasion of much teaching (6:34), but Mark has not given it, probably because Peter did not tell it. However, the power of Christ is revealed in the miracle and in the walking on the water. Jesus taught the disciples how to face great problems and to be of cheer in time of stress and strain.

113

6. *A Revolutionary Discourse.*—Chapter 7 gives one of the revolutionary discourses of Jesus when he accused the Pharisees of preferring tradition to truth and twitted them with their hypocritical practice of "Corban." The doctrine that not ceremonial contaminations but only the sinful thoughts of the heart really defile a man astonished even the disciples so much that they interviewed Jesus privately about it. Peter's amazement lasted until his experience on the housetop at Joppa (Acts 10), and Mark notes what Jesus said to the disciples "making all meats clean" (7:19). In 7:27 Jesus proclaimed to the Syrophenician woman the doctrine that the gospel comes to the Jew first. He tested her and then granted her request. Jesus knew that he was to be the Saviour of the world, but the Chosen People had the first privilege.

In 8:2 f. Christ showed his pity for the multitudes. For three days they had been with Jesus listening to his teaching. Now he desired to feed their stomachs as well as their souls, lest they faint on the way. It is good to use the kitchen as well as the pulpit, if one does not let the soup kitchen take the place of the gospel. Christ first fed their hearts and then satisfied their hunger out of pity. We are prone to use hunger as a bit to entice men to hear the gospel.

7. *Confessing His Messiahship.*—Jesus had much to try his spirit. The captious criticism of his enemies made Christ refuse to perform signs to order, especially signs from heaven to conform to their theological implications about the messiahship (8:11 f.). The dulness of the disciples distressed Jesus greatly when they took his parable about the leaven of the Pharisees and the leaven of Herod literally (8:15 ff.), an absolutely jejune performance. Jesus took them to task sharply for intellectual inertness (8:17-21). Every teacher has his times of discouragement when it seems useless to go on. But better days come to us all, as

114

they did to Jesus. Near Caesarea Philippi, Jesus tested his disciples concerning their opinion of him. People had various ideas of Jesus then, but Peter spoke up for the twelve and said, "Thou art the Christ" (8:29). Jesus was pleased at the confession, though he urged them not to tell it publicly.

John's Gospel shows that Jesus revealed himself to some as the Messiah at the beginning of his work. The public announcement of this fact, however, came at the end of his ministry and helped to precipitate the crisis, as Jesus foresaw it would. The value of the confession of the disciples "is in the fact that it is not their assent to his claim, but their estimate of his greatness. They, as Jews, had inherited an idea, an expectation of a man in whom human greatness would culminate. . . . The race has culminated in him, and he is therefore the Messiah whom we are to expect."

8. *Foretelling His Death.*—Jesus had reached a crisis in his work, and the disciples are true to him even after the great Galilean defection. They are now in a position to be told the truth about the cross of Christ, his sacrificial death as the Saviour from sin. "And he began to teach them, that the Son of man must suffer many things, and be rejected by the elders, and the chief priests, and the scribes, and be killed, and after three days rise again" (8:31). The time had come, "and he spake the saying openly." A surgeon often probes deep enough to find inflammation where all seemed to be healed over. "And Peter took him, and began to rebuke him." Peter could not bear to have Jesus interfere with his messianic theology by talking about his death. That to Peter spoiled everything, absolutely everything, for he still had the pharisaic notion of a political Messiah and kingdom.

The word of Jesus cut Peter to the quick: "Get thee behind me, Satan; for thou mindest not the things of God, but the things of men" (8:33). Dazed as Peter was, it is doubtful if he grasped clearly the profound words of Jesus that followed concerning the philosophy of life and death, of finding life in death and death in life. And yet he treasured them in his memory until he did understand them, and Mark wrote them down. One may gain the whole world and forfeit one's soul, like the madness of Alexander the Great or Napoleon. The Son of man is the judge of this world, and he will be ashamed of those who are ashamed of him (8:38).

9. *Eschatology.*—The words of Jesus in 9:1 have puzzled many. What did Jesus mean by those still living who would see the kingdom of God come with power? The transfiguration, his own resurrection, Pentecost, the destruction of Jerusalem, the second coming? Each view has its difficulties. We have come upon the eschatology of Jesus, a theme that bristles with difficulties. Schweitzer makes eschatology the chief thing in the teaching of Jesus. He is thus a mere apocalyptical dreamer with only "interim" ethics and no world program.

We are face to face with the question of whether or not Jesus had adopted the cataclysmic view of the current Jewish apocalyptists and expected a sudden demonstration of power that never came and a personal return within that generation. In a word, we are asked to believe that Jesus was grievously mistaken in the very thing concerning which he claimed superior knowledge, the kingdom of God. He did use apocalyptic imagery, as in chapter 13, the so-called "little apocalypse," and the Sermon on the Mount, in which he foretold the destruction of Jerusalem and finally the end of the world. The language is symbolic and highly figurative, but Jesus expressly disclaimed knowledge of the time of the end of the world (13:32), and that makes us wonder if he could have had that idea in mind in 9:1 and

116

in 13:30. We have not reached the end of this debate, but the eschatological side of Christ's teaching in the apocalyptic form must not be made the major thing in his teaching to the neglect of the ethical and clearly spiritual notes which we can understand.

We have no word from Jesus on the Mount of Transfiguration, but he manifested keen disappointment at the failure of the disciples to cure the epileptic boy while he was on the mountain (9:19) and told the father that faith is the door to all power (9:23)—faith and prayer (9:29), which the disciples had omitted, obvious explanation of much failure today on the part of workers for Christ.

10. *Practical Ethics in the Light of the Cross.*—The time drew nearer when Jesus must make plain the fact of his coming death (9:30–32). Not only did the disciples not understand his teaching on this point but they apparently took no interest in it, for they were bent on settling their own rank so as to be ready for the chief places in the political kingdom which they expected the Messiah to set up (9:33–37). Jesus made service the test of greatness and childlikeness the mark of discipleship. The rebuke of John's narrowness is pertinent today when men are often overzealous about punctilios and partisanship overtops loyalty to Christ.

The position of Christ on marriage and divorce is challenged by many today as then. Easy divorce has always been popular in times of loose living. Mark (10:5–12) does not give the one ground for divorce found in Matthew 5:32 and 19:9, and Mark quotes Christ as forbidding wives to divorce their husbands. Only Jewish women of prominence could do that, women like Salome, Herod's sister, and Herodias. Christ's love for little children is shown by his tender words in 10:14 ff., and his love for a young man in the grip of a great sin appears in 10:21. Jesus spoke plainly

117

about the terrible power of money over men's lives (10:23–31). His words amazed Peter and the rest, but in our age of materialism it is easy enough to see the point.

The plain prediction of the death of Jesus still failed to impress the disciples, for James and John came right up to ask for the chief places in the kingdom. But at least we get from the incident the profound words of Jesus concerning his atoning death as the crowning illustration of devoted service for others (10:32–45), words whose depth we still cannot fathom.

Faith made blind Bartimeus whole, Jesus said (10:52), and faith can remove mountains still (11:23–25), faith coupled with the forgiving spirit. Jesus purposely proclaimed himself Messiah by the triumphal entry and claimed messianic power in cleansing the Temple (11:17). Nowhere does the mastery of Christ stand out more clearly than in the wonderful debate on the Tuesday of Passion Week when Jesus routed his enemies in a series of attacks in the Temple (11:27–44). Pharisees, Sadducees, Herodians, the Sanhedrin, and students all went down before the storm and fury of Christ's withering words. The more they winced, the more the common people rejoiced, and Christ remained the master teacher of the Temple, to the rage of his foes.

The eschatological discourse on the Mount of Olives (chap. 13) followed on that same afternoon, with its wondrous picture of the woes impending upon Jerusalem and the warning against that day of doom and the remote judgment of the world. The apocalyptic language symbolizes the power of Christ. We falter as we seek to interpret these symbols, but we must not rob them of all pith and point.

11. *The Sacrificial Aspect of Christ's Death.*—Mary of Bethany alone showed insight concerning Christ's death, and he defended her deed in words of immortal sympathy that angered Judas and spurred him on to make his hellish

compact with the puzzled ecclesiastics (14:1–11). But Jesus did not hesitate to point out the betrayer during the last Passover meal, though the rest seemed not to have grasped the signal (14:12–21). The words of Christ in the institution of the Lord's Supper plainly show that Christ was conscious of the sacrificial aspect of his atoning death for the sins of men (14:22–25). The warning to Peter brought only boasting (14:27–31), and the privilege of watching with Christ in his agony in the garden found the chosen three inert in body and unable to keep awake while the Son of man writhed on the ground with the load of the sins of mankind. The cry for help to the Father was wrung from the broken, but not rebellious, heart of God's Son, who submitted wholly to the Father's will (14:32–40).

Jesus met his betrayal, arrest, trial, and crucifixion with an air of innocence and of triumph (14:41 to 15:37). He was fully aware that he voluntarily surrendered his life for the life of men, and his courage to the end was not really marred by the cry of loneliness after three hours of darkness when he felt so keenly that the Father had withdrawn for the moment his conscious presence (15:34). Jesus on oath before the Sanhedrin claimed to be the Messiah, the Son of God (14:61 f.), but he also claimed that though they killed him he would come in glory on the clouds and judge the whole earth.

Thus it will be seen that while Mark's Gospel does give only occasional sayings of Christ in connection with the historical occasions that called them forth, it in no wise gives a "reduced" Christianity. These extracts have the same flavor that we find in Matthew, Luke, John, and Paul. The "samples" prove the quality of the whole. The teaching of Jesus in Mark's Gospel is clear and consistent concerning the Father, the Son, sin, salvation, the kingdom, and the moral regeneration of men.

X

Aramaic and Latin Terms in Mark's Gospel

Abba, Father. MARK 14:36.

1. *Mark's Habit as Interpreter.*—The presence of Aramaic translations in Mark's Gospel has been used as proof that he wrote originally in that language. But the use of both transliteration and translation seems to show that the book was written originally in Greek. We know from Papias that Mark was Peter's interpreter or dragoman and was equally at home in both Aramaic and Greek, while Peter usually spoke in Aramaic. It seems likely that Mark's habit of translating for Peter's discourses crops out in the Gospel which was probably written in the current Greek.

2. *Proper Names.*—It is interesting to note these Aramaic terms and the circumstances connected with their use. Some of them are in Mark alone, some in Matthew, Luke, and John, but Mark has more of them, and several times he both transliterates and translates. Mark has the Aramaic form of some proper names, like Simon the Cananean (3:18, Zealot in Luke 6:14). Golgotha (15:22; Matt. 27:33) is translated both in Matthew and Mark as "the place of a skull," while Luke (23:33) has only "the place which is called The skull" (like Latin Calvary), and John (19:17) has "the place called The place of a skull, which is called

in Hebrew Golgotha." It is not surprising that the Gospels all seek to locate carefully the scene of the tragedy of the cross on the hill which looks like a skull just to the north of Jersualem.

3. *Boanerges.*—In 3:17 Mark says that Jesus surnamed James and John "Boanerges," which is "sons of thunder." It is not said that Jesus gave them this nickname at the time that they were chosen as apostles. We know that later James and John wished to call down fire from heaven on the Samaritan village that did not receive Christ kindly and were sternly rebuked by Jesus (Luke 9:52–55). This explosive trait in the two brothers appears also in the impulsive request that they be given the two chief places in Christ's kingdom (Mark 10:35 ff.; Matt. 20:20 ff.). Mark alone has preserved the word "Boanerges" as applied by Christ to them, but Justin Martyr says that in Peter's "memoirs" of Jesus is recorded the fact that Jesus "named the two sons of Zebedee 'Boanerges,' which means 'sons of thunder.'" Mark's Gospel was sometimes called Peter's "Memorabilia of Jesus."

4. *Talitha cumi.*—In 5:41 we have another instance of the Aramaic transliteration. There is a tender touch of pathos in the preservation of the very words used by Jesus as he stood by the bedside of the twelve-year-old daughter of Jairus. The message had already come to Jesus that the child was dead and that he need not trouble further about the case (Mark 5:35 f.), but Jesus disregarded the word and urged the ruler, "Fear not, only believe." He took along with him Peter, James, and John. The crowd of mourners "laughed him to scorn" when Jesus insisted that "the child is not dead, but sleepeth." Mark is never more graphic than in the following verse: "But he, having put them all forth, taketh the father of the child and her mother and them that were with him, and goeth in where the child was."

Peter was in that chamber of death and now for the first time saw Jesus raise the dead. He remembered Christ's very words as "taking the child by the hand, he saith unto her, *Talitha cumi.*" Jesus used either Greek or Aramaic as occasion required. Here he spoke in Aramaic, and these are the very words which he employed, just these two words. *Talitha* means "maid," and *cumi* means "arise." Mark heard Peter tell the story and kept the Aramaic language of Jesus but took pains to translate it in Greek for the benefit of his many readers who did not know the Aramaic, just as John translated the Aramaic titles "rabbi" (1:38) and "Messiah" (1:41) and the name "Cephas" (1:42). The chamber of death became the chamber of life, for Jesus was in it, and joy took the place of grief in that home.

5. *Corban.*—Once again Mark retains the Aramaic word *Corban* and explains it as meaning "given to God" (7:11). Matthew (15:5) has only the translation. Peter was present on that occasion when Jesus so powerfully exposed the hollowness of the pharisaic traditionalism which put the tradition of the elders in the place of the Word of God, and "Peter answered and said unto him, Declare unto us the parable" (Matt. 15:15). Mark thus retains Christ's striking word which Peter remembered. The explanation by Jesus was particularly pertinent for Peter in view of his later experience at Joppa and at Caesarea (Acts 10). Mark (7:19) adds a suggestive anacoluthic clause: "Making all meats clean." Peter did not see it then, but he did afterwards. Mark may be here preserving Peter's own comment on the incident. The Jews had become so used to the pharisaic trickery called *Corban* that the exposure and denunciation of it seemed a breach of courtesy to the disciples (Matt. 15:12). Custom so easily and so quickly blinds the eyes to moral and spiritual reality that it becomes difficult for us to see things in a new light.

6. *Ephphatha.*—Another Aramaic word in Mark (7:34) is *Ephphatha* and means "be opened," as Mark explains in Greek. Here again the probability is that Mark is retaining Peter's verbatim report of the words of Jesus to the deaf and dumb man when he was healed. The notes of an eye-witness are present in Mark's report here. Jesus "took him aside from the multitude privately," as he often did, particularly when he wished to avoid public commotion as here in the borders of Decapolis. Mark gives the various details, how Jesus "put his fingers into his ears," as if to awaken the sense of hearing. Then "he spat, and touched his tongue," as if again to help the man by suggestion. Then "looking up to heaven, he sighed, and saith unto him, Ephphatha, that is, Be opened." Evidently Peter told this incident with vividness. Mark sees the picture and makes us see it. The cure was instantaneous, and Jesus charged the witnesses to tell no man, "but the more he charged them, so much the more a great deal they published it" (7:36), a bit of nature not unknown today.

In Mark 9:5 we have the Aramaic *Rabbi* (my honorable sir) without translation into Greek, where Matthew (17:4) has "Lord" and Luke (9:33) has "Master." In Matthew 23:8 "Rabbi" is translated "Teacher," as "Rabboni" is in John 20:16. Mark has "Rabboni" in 10:51, according to the correct text, though in the margin we find "Lord, Rabbi."

7. *Bartimeus.*—Mark alone preserves the redundant Bartimeus, "the son of Timaeus" (10:46). Here again Peter's quick ear and love of detail caught and held the name of this blind beggar "sitting by the way side," as Mark pictures him. Mark 11:9, like Matthew 21:9, retains the Aramaic "hosanna" of the exultant throng as they marched into Jerusalem.

8. *Abba, Father.*—Once more it is Mark who gives us "Abba, Father," from the lips of Jesus as he "fell on

123

the ground, and prayed that, if it were possible, the hour might pass from him" (14:36). Matthew has "My Father" (26:39), and Luke has "Father" (22:42). It is not certain that we have here transliteration and translation as in some other instances in Mark. It is quite possible that here Jesus himself uttered both words, the Aramaic *Abba* and the Greek *Pater*, somewhat like our "Papa, Father." In moments of great emotion the language of childhood comes back to us with tremendous meaning. Twice we find Paul using this very combination in referring to God. In both instances he gives us the language of childhood. Paul was bilingual, as was Jesus. In Galatians 4:6 it is God's Spirit (the Spirit of God's Son) teaching our hearts to cry, "Abba, Father," and to feel the joy of sonship. In Romans 8:15 it is the spirit of adoption that leads us to look up to God as Father and lovingly say, "Abba, Father." But, all the more, we see how Mark has given us the very words that burst from the heart of Jesus in his hour of great agony in the garden of Gethsemane.

9. *Eloi, Eloi.*—In Mark 15:34 we have the Aramaic word from the cross, in contrast with the Hebrew form in Matthew 27:46. In both instances the translation is given. Jesus almost certainly cried out after the three hours of dreadful darkness and unbearable silence in the Aramaic. The Hebrew "Eli" sounds more like "Elijah," as some misunderstood Jesus, than the Aramaic "Eloi." But it was a misapprehension in either case. One can almost hear that cry of protest against the burden of the world's sin on his soul as the Father for the moment veiled his face. Jesus had always until now been able to find comfort and understanding in the Father who now seemed to have left him, even reproached him, as some manuscripts have it. No wail of woe was ever so bitter as this. Jesus was drinking his cup to the very bottom.

10. *Latin Words.*—Some scholars argue that Mark wrote his Gospel first in Latin, because he was in Rome and because he has some Latin words in the book. A few of the late manuscripts of the Gospel also affirm in the subscriptions that Mark wrote in Latin. He probably knew Latin as did Paul, but it is highly improbable that he wrote in Latin. Greek was the language in current use over the empire and in Rome itself outside of the official documents. Marcus Aurelius wrote his *Meditations* in Greek. Paul wrote to the church in Rome in Greek. There are a few more Latin words in Mark than in the other Gospels, but this is only natural if he was in Rome. They are all political, military, or monetary words, only the ones that would permeate the current Greek. So we find denarius (6:37), centurion (15:39, 44), quadrans (12:42), pallet or camp bed (2:4, 9, 11), legion (5:9, 15), sextarius, wooden pitcher for measuring liquids (7:4), spy or scout, speculator (6:27).

Mark wrote in the vernacular Greek of the period, the *koine*, but was undoubtedly at home in the Aramaic (his native tongue) and probably had an acquaintance with the official Latin. He was a practical linguist, not a technical expert. He has given us the language of the life of the times and some actual transliterations of the Aramaic words of Jesus our Lord.

XI

The Disputed Close
of Mark's Gospel

And they said nothing to any one; for they were
afraid.   MARK 16:8,

1. *Interpolations in the New Testament.*—Textual criticism is considered a dry subject by most people, whether it be concerned with the text of Homer, Shakespeare, or Mark, but it is a necessary science. There are many who recall the sensation created when the Revised Version was printed without John 5:4 (the angel stirring the water), Acts 8:37 (the demand for the eunuch's confession), and 1 John 5:7–8 (the famous passage about the Trinity). And yet no one today dares claim the genuineness of these passages, which are found in the *Textus Receptus.* The addition in 1 John 5:7–8, according to Gregory in his *Canon and Text of the New Testament,* "never was a part of the Greek New Testament and should be omitted from it as if Erasmus had never been brought to print it. It should be left out without word or sign that any false word ever had been there."

It seems reasonably certain also that John 7:53 to 8:11 (the story of the woman taken in adultery) is not a part of the Gospel of John. The evidence against it is overwhelming, and yet it is almost certainly a true incident. The verdict of Gregory may be accepted again: "I do not doubt that this story is a true story and that it has exercised its charm in oral and then in written tradition since the day on which the woman stood before Jesus." We must remember that the gospels do not undertake to tell all that Jesus did and said. There are numerous interpolations in various manuscripts of the New Testament, some of them very interesting. It would be no wonder that during the long centuries some scribes made marginal notes that crept into the text. D. L. Moody marked his Bible from end to end. It is one of the treasures to see at Northfield. The great number of Greek manuscripts of the New Testament, some of them very early, make it possible to eliminate most of the additions with great ease.

2. *The Difficulty About Mark 16:9–20.*—This is the chief textual problem in the Gospel of Mark and, one may add, in the New Testament itself. The length of it makes the loss of it serious, and it seems to leave the Gospel a torso. A long and furious battle has raged round this problem, the smoke of which may be said to have finally cleared away. Great scholars championed its genuineness, such men as Bengel, Eichhorn, Scholz, De Wette, Olshausen, Bleek, Lange, Ebrard, Scrivener, Canon Cook, Salmon, E. Miller, Belser, and in particular Dean Burgon, who thought that his book, *The Last Twelve Verses of S. Mark,* settled the problem. "He assailed those who were for removing these verses from the text, and, as he believed, smote his antagonists hip and thigh with a great slaughter." But critical scholars have found it very hard to get away from the calm and judicial survey of all the facts by Hort in his "Notes on Select Readings" (pp. 28–51), *Introduction and Appendix to the New Testament in the Original Greek,* in which he sums up his argument against the genuineness of Mark 16:9–20 but holds that it is a very early addition. Gregory

is positive that textual criticism has shown that this passage has "no right to a place in the text of the New Testament." John A. Broadus held that the problem had not been solved but that at least the passage was too doubtful to use in exposition as authoritative. Let us, then, see precisely what the situation is. There is a positive romance about the close of Mark's Gospel.

3. *The Short Ending.*—Did Mark's Gospel end at 16:8? If so, it ended thus: "And they went out, and fled from the tomb; for trembling and astonishment had come upon them: and they said nothing to any one; for they were afraid." Surely this is an astonishing conclusion for a Gospel that tells the story of the risen Christ. There are many scholars who argue that the abrupt "for they were afraid" could not possibly be the end of the Gospel, for it seems to be only part of a sentence. J. Rendel Harris is sure that two more words were written by Mark anyhow: "I am not going to speculate on these matters further than to tell you the first two words that will be found on the missing leaf, if it should ever be recovered. The narrative went on like this: (For they were afraid) of the Jews."

However, it is possible that the Gospel did end at verse 8. It may be argued that the very abruptness of the ending points to an early date when, in light of the resurrection and the eager expectation of the Parousia, no need would be felt for any subsequent history. What we must say in the light of textual criticism is that none of the various additions to verse 8 can possibly be a part of the original Gospel.

The evidence for the short ending is strong. The two oldest and best Greek manuscripts of the New Testament, Aleph (Codex Sinaiticus) and B (Codex Vaticanus), stop with verse 8. B has a blank space, which shows that the scribe knew of the longer ending but concluded not to give it. The Sinaitic Syriac stops also at this point, as does the margin of the Harclean Syriac. The best manuscripts of the Armenian and some of the older Ethiopic manuscripts likewise end with verse 8. Eusebius says that "almost all the Greek copies" are without further ending. Victor of Antioch, who wrote the earliest known commentary on Mark, stops his comment with verse 8.

Some of the Greek manuscripts (cursives) that give the longer ending say that it is not found in other manuscripts. The cursive Greek manuscript 22 marks "End" after verse 8, according to some of the copies, but adds that in many the regular ending is found. Similar comments appear in 1, 20, and nearly thirty other cursives. L gives two other endings and so really favors neither, though apparently not satisfied to stop at verse 8. Thus a very strong case is made for having no ending other than 16:8. And yet one cannot help wondering if something has not happened, if Mark really meant to end his Gospel here.

4. *The Intermediate Ending.*—Four Greek uncial manuscripts (L, 044, 099, 0112), the Greek cursive 274 (margin), the Old Latin k, the manuscripts of the Memphitic, and several of the Ethiopic manuscripts give the following for Mark's Gospel after 16:8: "And they reported briefly to Peter and those in his company all the things commanded. And after these things Jesus himself also sent forth through them from the East even to the West the holy and incorruptible message of eternal salvation." The four uncials belong to the eighth and ninth centuries, and L is the only one of value. L actually has two endings added after verse 8. It is evident that the scribe intends the Gospel to end there but adds the two endings known to be current. The other manuscripts also give the ending above as an alternative to the long ending (the *Textus Receptus*). The Old Latin k has this intermediate ending alone. It is quite evident that

129

it was originally written as a conclusion to the Gospel of Mark and is not an independent fragment. Apparently the archetype of L and the related manuscripts ended at verse 8 with "for they were afraid." The scribes have added the two endings with which they were familiar from other manuscripts, preferring the shorter one which they have placed first. This little paragraph does bear some resemblance to Luke's prologue (1:1–4), and its date may be early. It is, however, clearly inferior to the longer ending and was soon abandoned. However, since no one now holds it to be genuine, we need not tarry longer over it.

5. *An Expansion of the Long Ending.*—The Washington manuscript of the Gospel (W) has "after Mark 16:14 a remarkable apocryphal addition, hitherto only partially known from a reference in Jerome." So Kenyon describes the rather startling expansion in this manuscript (Freer Gospels or W), which has given a new turn to the discussion concerning the close of Mark's Gospel. America has reason to be proud of the possession of this valuable document, due to the generosity of Mr. C. L. Freer, of Detroit. The manuscript is to be dated in the fourth or fifth century and contains this addition to the long ending of Mark:

And they defended themselves, saying: This world of lawlessness and of unbelief is under Satan, which does not suffer those unclean things that are under the dominion of spirits to comprehend the true powers of God. On this account reveal thy righteousness now. They said (these things) to Christ. And Christ replied to them: There has been fulfilled the term of years of the authority of Satan, but other dreadful things are drawing nigh (even to those) for the sake of whom as sinners I was delivered up to death in order that they might inherit the spiritual and incorruptible glory of righteousness which is in heaven.

No one maintains that this rather florid passage belongs to the original Mark nor even to the original form of the long ending of the *Textus Receptus*. Kenyon seems justified in aligning it with the apocryphal additions. It does not stand in the same category as John 7:53 to 8:11, which is almost certainly a true incident. It is evidently a marginal note which crept into the text at an early date. In the Washington manuscript the order of the Gospels is Matthew, John, Luke, Mark.

6. *The Long Ending.*—This is the current text for Mark 16:9–20 as we have it in our editions of the New Testament.

With the exception of Aleph, and B, which have no ending, and L, 044, 099, 0112, which have both endings, the longer ending follows verse 8 without a break in every known Greek manuscript outside of the cursives mentioned above. It appears in the most of the Old Latin manuscripts, in the Curetonian Syriac, in the Memphitic, and in the Gothic versions. Irenaeus quotes verse 19 as part of the Gospel of Mark, and thereafter it is frequently referred to by Christian writers. This mass of external testimony for the longer ending is not, however, conclusive proof of its genuineness. Manuscripts have to be weighed and not merely counted. Any passage in the Gospels that is not supported by Aleph and B, L, Sinaitic Syriac, k of the Old Latin manuscripts is far from having it all one way. Besides, the existence of two of these added endings (really three, counting the logion in the Washington manuscript) discredits each of them.

When the external evidence is classified by Westcott and Hort, dropping out of the Syrian class of late documents and admitting mixture between the Alexandrian and the Western classes, we have at bottom a conflict between the Neutral and the Western classes, with the presumption in favor of the Neutral class (Aleph, B, L).

When we turn to internal evidence, the case against the passage is very much strengthened, proving conclusively that these verses could not have been written by Mark. Verses 8 and 9 do not really fit together. This closing paragraph has a number of non-Marcan words. These are Johannine but not Marcan. The style is less vivid and more didactic. There is every evidence, therefore, that we have here an independent composition, a sort of early epitome of the appearance of Jesus, after the order of the documents used by Luke to which he refers in his Gospel, 1:1–4.

So far, critics had come with surprising unanimity when, as Swete says, "In November 1891 Mr E. C. Conybeare found in the Patriarchal Library of Edschmiatzin an Armenian MS. of the Gospels written A.D. 986, in which the last twelve verses of St Mark are introduced by a rubric written in the first hand, *Of the presbyter Ariston.*" Who is this "presbyter Ariston" who is here said to be the author of the long ending of Mark's Gospel? The usual interpretation today is that the Armenian scribe had in mind the Aristion whom Papias mentioned in connection with the Presbyter John (probably the apostle John). If so, then this appendix comes from a disciple of the apostle John, and the Johannine style is explained. Many scholars agree that we have at last found the author of this addition, although some still prefer to think of an unnamed writer of the early period. Salmon pleads that "we must ascribe the authorship to one who lived in the very first age of the Church. And why not St. Mark?" To be sure, if Mark made several editions of his Gospel, he may have added this ending to the last one. But even so, there would still be the difference in style to explain. The notion that the Petrine material gave out at 16:8 assumes that Peter wrote out his recollections, which is not what tradition says about it.

7. *A Lost Ending.*—So far we have considered the possibility that Mark's Gospel stopped at 16:8 without further ending. But Rendel Harris will have none of that:

We are aware now that the Gospel is shorn of its last twelve verses and ends abruptly with the words 'And they were afraid' —which is not a literary ending nor a Christian ending and can hardly be a Greek ending: so that we are obliged to assume that the real ending of Mark is gone, and speculate as we please as to what has become of it and what it was like.

I do not myself feel quite so sure as Dr. Harris that the Gospel did not end with 16:8. It may not be literary and it is rather free Greek (vernacular Koine such as Mark used), but it is certainly Christian, for it establishes the fact of Christ's resurrection with the restoration of Peter to favor. The fear of the women does make a rather depressing close, but we do not know what Mark's motives were, if he closed here. It is possible, of course, that Mark meant to write more and never did, being interrupted by a journey or even by death. It is possible that the last leaf of the autograph was lost before there were any copies made of it. In the papyrus roll the outside leaf would be the first to be torn off. It is common enough with us for the last leaf of paper-bound books to be lost. Warfield writes,

Why Mark's Gospel has come down to us incomplete, we do not know. Was Mark interrupted at this point by arrest or martyrdom before he finished his book? Was a page lost off the autograph itself? Or do all of our witnesses carry us back only to a mutilated copy short of the autograph, the common original of all of them, so that our oldest transmitted text is sadly different from the original text?

Shall we stop with this critical impasse? The intermediate ending is no longer defended by anyone as genuine. The time is fast approaching when the same can be said of the more familiar longer ending. We must treat the longer ending as instructive but not a part of Mark's Gospel. Gregory writes, "A Christian may read, enjoy, ponder them, and be thankful for them as much as he pleases."

Is it possible that the genuine ending of Mark will some day be recovered? Who can tell? Stranger things have already taken place in modern research. If Mark did write more for his Gospel and if copies were made of the autograph before it perished and before that leaf or leaves disappeared, then some day we may see the true ending of Mark's Gospel.